BLACKPOOL

John Craven
WING HALF

Conker Editions Ltd
22 Cosby Road
Littlethorpe
Leicester
LE19 2HF
Email: books@conkereditions.co.uk
Website: www.conkereditions.co.uk
First published by Conker Editions Ltd 2021
Text © 2021 Roy Calley.

A CIP catalogue record for this book is available from the British Library.
13-digit ISBN: 978-1-9999008-7-8
Design and typesetting by Gary Silke.
Printed in the UK by Mixam.

FLAT CAPS & TANGERINE SCARVES

Roy Calley

CONKER

Prologue

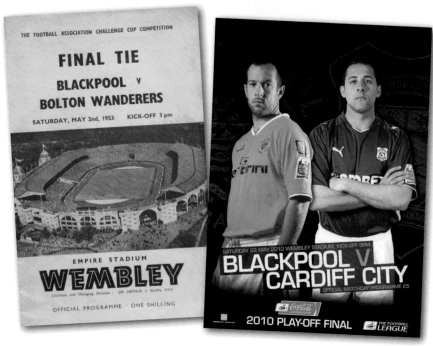

C lose your eyes. Breathe. Close your eyes and breathe. Try to empty your mind and let yourself relax. Calm. Quiet. Let nothing enter you and disturb this moment. This is special. Whatever you have done in the past, it does not count. This is where you should be at this moment, at this time. Do not let it get to you. Remember to be in control. You try yet it won't work, and it doesn't work.

No matter how hard you try to slow your body down and count the heartbeats so that they strike normally, the spirit refuses to obey. You're on the edge. You're at the limit already. There's no ignoring this moment. The calmness is overwhelmed by the adrenaline, the excitement, the apprehension, the fear.

The noise is there, although gentle at first, like a whisper in the ear. At first, it's just the almost-silent sound of others in their rituals. Shaking their arms, *bouncing up and down on their toes, flexing their fingers. Small sounds of breathing, rhythmic inner chants of self-confidence and self-challenge. Then you notice the sounds of studded boots on the concrete floor and padded shoes on the carpet, some heavy but some so light as to be almost imperceptible. Then there's a shout. It's almost anguished but it's noticeable. A cry to arms, a shout of encouragement. You're not sure where or who it's come from, but it's there and it adds to the tension.*

Soon you hear the sounds from the front. It's odd that you've not noticed before, but they are there, like someone opening a door to the outside. It's now not possible not to notice. It's too loud, it's too insistent. The crowd, firstly singing to some tune that you know but at this moment can't place, then the cries of support, a mass of noise that assaults your senses. There are many in the crowd and they are waiting, impatiently, expectantly. Now you open your eyes.

In front and behind are your team-mates and, next to you, the men you have to overpower. Each one of them experiencing their own moment of solitude, their own personal agony, but all comfortable in the knowledge that it's shared. At the front is the man who has done so much to make this happen. His smile is permanent, but it's a fixed and scared smile. There's a light in front of him where the tunnel ends, almost making silhouettes of each jumping, shouting, flexing and nervous player. It's surreal and, for a brief second, you wonder how on earth you got here. Then there's the fear. There are people, not just fans but family also, who are watching. They are hoping, praying, crossing fingers, closing eyes and hugging each other as the true moment arrives. Then it's time. The signal, and you all move forward in unison. Quiet and noisy at the same time. Nervous glances and bravado. Don't fail me now. Don't let this overwhelm me. Only then, when you walk into the light and the crescendo hits you, do you really and truly realise what is about to happen.

The tangerine shirts glisten in the sunlight. The white shirts opposite reflect and temporarily blind you. The white shirts cool you. The blue shirts opposite already absorbing the heat. It's Wembley. Two moments, two separate eras, but one football club.

Introduction

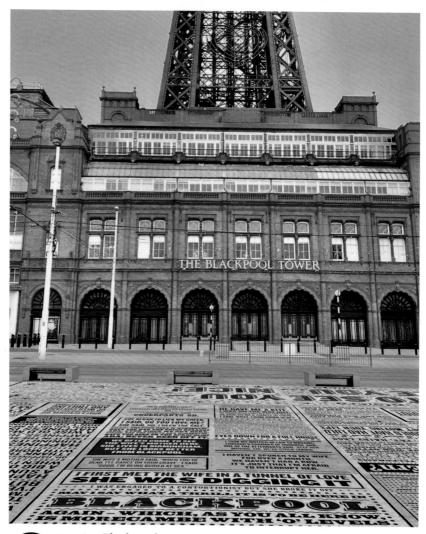

Opposite Blackpool Tower, on the newly renovated promenade, there is a large square of engravings set into the concrete called 'The Comedy Carpet'. This is comprised of 850 jokes and witty sentences from comedians and actors who have appeared in the town, some funny, some amusing, some slightly less so. It's a perfect microcosm of a seaside resort that has ebbed and flowed in popularity for over a century, the ribald humour and the saucy postcard epitomising what Blackpool is all about. A good hour can be spent standing and reading and smiling, providing the Irish Sea gales aren't at their worst and you can avoid the families, cyclists and holidaymakers. With the exception of the sandy beach, it's just about the only free form of entertainment in the town.

If you then head south, passing the 'bed and breakfast' hotels offering 'en-suite' and 'satellite TV', the numerous Gypsy Rose stalls and the gaudy souvenir shops with Spanish sombreros and pink candy floss, the sea cascading against the concrete barriers and the three piers reaching out to the horizon, you soon arrive at the Manchester Bar. This has been a geographical landmark for over a century, and it stands as a testament to the year-passing similarity, and also the ever-changing façade that Blackpool shows to the world. It corners the promenade and a busy Lytham Road, which makes its razor-straight way to the South Shore area of Blackpool. It is on this road that the harsh reality of a town that relies almost exclusively on the economic benefits of the tourist trade becomes apparent. Boarded-up shops, run-down living accommodation and a sense of decay greets the unwary. Thankfully, the sight of Bloomfield Road appearing on the left means that there isn't much reason to linger, and this is of course the home of Blackpool Football Club.

I mention this particular short-route because this is the one that thousands of tangerine-clad fans – old and young, male and female, families and couples – all made their way along, one windy but sunny day in March 2019. The promenade was closed briefly as the mass of supporters chanting 'Blackpool are back' finally converged at a place they had almost completely boycotted for five years, a return to supporting their club after the departure of owners who seemed to embrace the word 'toxic'. The stadium was ready to welcome them back, seemingly gleaming in the sunlight, but wary of closer inspection.

The ground, the stadium, whatever title it has been given down the years, doesn't actually have a name. It's called Bloomfield Road because that's where it is (although, in its previous incarnation, it was referred to as 'Gamble's Field') and there are no tasteless sponsors attached or twice-a-decade name changes. It is simply Bloomfield Road. This is the place that has delighted, despaired, angered and confounded the supporters from the first day a bunch of eleven players ran on to the pitch representing the town of Blackpool. That is the point about the club. Supporting it is consigning a significant part of your life to the emotional 'rollercoaster' (predictable description) of highs and lows that can cause unhealthy levels of stress. It is not unique in that respect, as all fans of all clubs have seen the highs, and mostly lows, but Blackpool seems to embrace the word 'crisis', using it as a template for its existence. People say that you have to experience the lows to enjoy the highs, but 'sandgrown 'uns' tend to distrust the successes, knowing full well that the next set of failures is just a foolish decision away. Not for them the vagaries of the inconsistent whistle-blowing referee, or the last-minute heartbreaker. No, when Blackpool FC does a crisis, it does it properly and makes sure the whole world is aware of the heart-wrenching, soul-destroying nature of the latest calamity to befall a club that is regularly portrayed as the 'nation's second favourite'.

It is a community club. That is the way it is portrayed in this new era of football watching, but whereas the community has at times followed it with something bordering on obsession, they have also at other times turned their backs on it. From packing the promenade to welcome back the promotion heroes of 2010, to the crumbling relic of a ground where fewer than 2,000 stood to witness a League game. The ground stands as an icon of hope or as a shudder of embarrassment, depending on the era you were living in.

This is a club that has feasted at the top table and then, within the blinking of an eye, found itself scrabbling for the scraps left on the floor. A former Blackpool player during the Second World War, Bill Beckett, once said that the First Division without Blackpool was like having 'strawberries without cream'; but that particular delicacy was never associated with the gruff northern town, brought up on fish and chips and bitter ale, and the cream would by now have curdled. Despite being one of the most famous clubs in the land, they have only eaten at the high table once in the past 50 years, but they certainly made a feast of it.

This is not bitter rivals Preston North End or Burnley or Blackburn Rovers. They have their moments, of course, but for the most part they live their footballing lives in a calm and orderly fashion, occasionally giving their seaside neighbours a curious and knowing glance as the mischievous tangerines create a stir again. This is a club that brought legendary manager Billy Ayre close to tears as he stood on the Wembley turf as the midnight hour approached and said that he'd 'not had a worse moment in his life, never mind football'. A club that three seasons later, completed the most astonishing capitulation when a near mathematical impossibility was achieved and promotion was

waved away. Two decades earlier they had missed promotion back to the First Division by 0.21 of a goal and then later sacked the manager. Not just any old manager, but one of the most famous players to wear a tangerine shirt. Just for measure, they did it again in the mid '70s when a talented squad had finally started to gel and had entertained the faithful with ten home goals in the previous two matches. The manager was sacked. The team were relegated from a position of promotion just four months previously. Also, let us not forget that this is a club that dismissed its most successful and longest-serving manager by registered post, on a Saturday morning, just hours after he had travelled with the team to a League game.

These things, of course, do not compare to the off-field activities in recent seasons. When newspaper headlines proclaim 'Blackpool Shower', and the term 'Judgement Day' is associated with tangerine banners, smoke bombs and anger, then you know there is something slightly different about this club. From the grainy black-and-white images of the most famous Cup Final victory and the vibrant kaleidoscope of the Premier League season, to the forbidding gloom of re-election and the dark clouds shadowing empty seats in a deserted stadium, it is what Blackpool Football Club is all about. It is all here.

The Beginning

When writing a history of anything, it is usual to start at the beginning. That is something I have done twice now with Blackpool Football Club, so you'll indulge me a little, please, if I digress quite a lot. A biography normally takes its course from start to finish, and in a way that's exactly what should happen with Blackpool, but the club is an ongoing project where the final act is unlikely to be played out, even if that ending has felt closer than it ever should have. This will not be a chronological list of facts and figures but a celebration of a club that has steadfastly refused to grow in size, having watched flat-capped, Woodbine-smoking men clap loudly and tangerine-scarved youths misbehave out of sight of parents. It has embraced the working class as they seek escape on the packed concrete terraces and watched bemused as the more vociferous resolutely stood firm and refused to accept the invitation to enter. The club has meant everything to everyone and at times nothing to many. It has threatened to leave without a backward glance but has relented when attention was bestowed on it. Blackpool Football Club is a cruel mistress, but then a loving, cherished partner when asked. No supporter would really want it to be any different, and besides, it is part of the make-up of the club to be difficult. Anyway, let us start at the beginning.

Blackpool in the 1870s was a place on the verge of a boom. Its identity was being decided, the seaside air was deemed to be of benefit to the working population, so the sleepy hamlet was being transformed in alarmingly quick time. A promenade was constructed, three piers with dance halls, entertainment centres and teashops appeared, and the introduction of an electric tramway was proposed. Little of this was for the locals, as they only numbered in the region of around 14,000, but rather for the holidaymakers who could now take advantage of the steam railway that was being extended from the original Preston to Kirkham line. Blackpool, still at this point Tower-less, was becoming an attraction that has never truly faded, though the genteel ambience promoted in early advertisements offers little insight into what the town would eventually be transformed into.

At the same time Blackpool was revealing itself to the world, the game of football was also becoming increasingly popular, especially in the north of England and Scotland. Clubs were forming and taking the game to a professionalism not seen during the era of combined football and rugby rules, before the inevitable split that saw two entirely separate sports grow and prosper. With Blackpool expanding at an unheard-of pace, it was predictable that a football club would be formed to represent the town. So, in 1887, that is exactly what happened.

As with all good stories, there is always an element of doubt over their origins. Dates can be changed, details altered, documents misread, and so it is with the origin of Blackpool Football Club. The accepted story, and this is about as close to fact as possible, is that it came about from a breakaway from the original St John's FC on 26th July 1887. That particular club had been in existence for about a decade, and had itself been born of the struggling Victoria FC – almost certainly the outfit referred to as 'Blackpool Football Club' in an official Blackburn Rovers history relating a game in 1880. After a breakaway, and numerous heated exchanges in the Stanley Arms Hotel, five members of St John's formed what we now know as Blackpool FC. With such a confusing and difficult birth, it is hardly surprising that the club should be the mischievous and errant child.

There is always a beginning to everything, and the beginning for Blackpool Football Club came at Chorley. On 17th September 1887, the first of the club's thousands of matches took place, and they won it 2-1. Few, if any, of the spectators present that day would have imagined that of the two fledgling clubs, the one bearing the red shirts (although this is conjecture as there was no reference to team colours in contemporary reports, and they were basically a combination of red-coloured separate jumpers owned by the players themselves) would be the ones who would have the greater impact on English football. For the record, the first goal scored for the club was by Hargreaves, described as 'a ponderous kick half the length of the field'. Blackpool Football Club had taken its first baby steps into the adult world of football, and to show their progressive intent, the team managed to win both the Fylde Cup and the Lancashire Junior Cup in that first, uncertain season. As has always been the case though, a sense of injustice surrounded the final of the latter when the club complained that the venue of Deepdale in Preston was hardly neutral when facing Preston St Joseph's. Showing resilience in the face of unfair odds is something that has become a character trait of Blackpool down the years, and in that first season they stood tall and defeated the Preston team 2-1, in any case. It was a good start.

What has also become a constant when talking about Blackpool FC is the state of their finances, which have fluctuated alarmingly, and so it is refreshing to see that on their first balance sheet for the season, there were incomings of 108 pounds, twelve shillings and tuppence, as opposed to outgoings of 103 pounds, fourteen shillings and ninepence. Without attempting to convert the original figures, it is still easy to see that a tidy profit was made, something that would have made a future owner present his most gleaming smile.

The eight seasons between the first game at Chorley and the club's appearance in the Football League were spent in the newly formed Lancashire League, Blackpool being one of the original members. It was successful with a Championship title in 1894 and four runners-up positions, but as they were competing locally against South Shore and Fleetwood Rangers, supporters had too many options and so attendances were never as high as desired. Even the local newspaper, the *Gazette & News*, made the comment that '...*it must be a hot-headed supporter of either South Shore or Fleetwood who will not admit that the Blackpool team is the strongest in the Fylde... the sooner the South Shore and Blackpool clubs are fused into one, the better it will be.*'

Progressive words, but it was still six years after that 1893 report before it became a reality. By that time, Blackpool FC had become a limited company, and mindful of their position of the 'big fish in a small pond', they made the obvious decision to apply to join the national Football League, the first of its kind in the world. It consisted of two divisions, both of 16 clubs, which would change over the years. Blackpool successfully applied in 1896 and, with the exception of one season, have been there ever since. The town was now so popular as a seaside resort – the Tower having opened just two years previously, then the tallest structure in the British Empire – it was believed that the football club would benefit from the influx of visitors. With a population of

around 45,000 and visitor numbers close to a quarter of a million, lured by the electric tramways, three piers and recently opened Winter Gardens complex, a successful League football club was essential, alongside the now independent cricket club. The cricket club stubbornly refused to be more than they promised, whilst the football club made a point of being more than was originally expected.

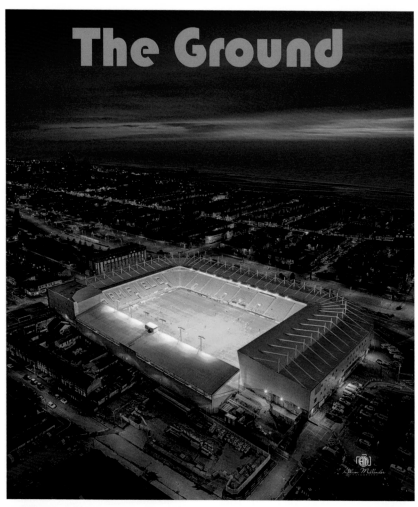

The Ground

The clock strikes, and you suddenly realise that it has moved too quickly. No time for another cup of tea. Outside, the sound of the rattling tram as it approaches. So, cap on head, a peck on the cheek and you jump on to the vehicle, panting and grinning as it pulls away from the stop. Only night-time games can do this. The wheels spark against the rails, yellow razor lights illuminating the dark, but soon dampened by the rain. The sea is angry tonight, it washes over the wall and caresses the promenade, but you have no time for such distractions. Tonight, it's the

Spurs in town. Fancy lads from the smoke. Our Billy and Jimmy will put paid to them. Bloomfield Road will never have looked so good.

At another time, the young boy, scarf hanging from his wrist, jumps on to the Number 6 bus and looks into the distance as the whiteness illuminates the sky above. On a night like this, the floodlights are more powerful than all the illuminations in their glory. His heart beats, a mixture of excitement and fear, the night preparing for him and the thousands of others. The game may be lost tonight, but the battle won't be. We'll make sure of that. His stomach churns a little. He'll need some chips and gravy to settle himself and then get on to the Kop. Let's hear the roar.

At a much later time, the old man walks slowly along the road, tangerine scarf wrapped around his neck to keep him warm, his eyes glistening. They glisten due to the iciness of the weather, but also as a silent cry for days long gone. Where did everyone go? This is not how it used to be, and it's not how it should be now. He feels alone, lost in the cavernous void left by the absence of the people he always relied on. The road is empty, the ground equally so, but the floodlights still shine.

Every entertainer needs a stage, and whether Blackpool are regarded as entertainers or not, they have their own theatre, and it is still called Bloomfield Road. There were two previous homes, Raikes Hall, or the Royal Palace Gardens as it was officially known, and the Athletic Grounds, now the site of Stanley Park. At the end of the 19th century though, the newly merged South Shore and Blackpool club (taking the Blackpool name) played its first game at 'Gamble's Field', as it had been known until then. Set in farmland, owned by a Mr Gamble, it was a warren of allotments and dusty tracks, hedges and railway sidings separating the western side from the seafront about a mile away. When South Shore had first played there just two months previously, the ground was not yet completed. It was reported in the local newspaper that '*the ground was not quite finished… and the linesman had plenty to do besides watching the game to keep the spectators from getting over the line. The grandstand was not up, but it is expected to be ready by next Saturday. A bar is being erected and two dressing tents.*'

By the time Blackpool played their first competitive fixture at the ground (an 8-0 victory over a ten-man Horwich RMI on 23rd December), these major plans had come to fruition, seemingly at a far quicker pace than improvements in later years. A 300-seater stand was built on the west side, with the noise of the trains behind, and white rope marked out the pitch and spectating area on the other three sides. It seemed a pretty comfortable, if not rather basic, environment for the club, but it didn't stop them from returning to Raikes Hall for a few months before finally making the decision to return to Bloomfield Road. Even then the ground wasn't regarded as being suitable for 'modern-day' football. After a game with Gainsborough Trinity, where a crowd of around 2,000 witnessed a 1-1 draw, the local newspaper made these rather scathing observations:

'Unfortunately for the club, the game had to be played at Bloomfield Road, and if there is one ground in this town that is unsuitable for the purpose for which it is used, then surely this is the one. It is out of the way... it was impossible to play on such a pitch, and the provision for the press was absolutely nil.'

These words could have been written at virtually any time in the club's history, but it meant a return to Raikes Hall and not returning to Bloomfield Road until the start of the 1901-02 season, after certain improvements had been made, although they weren't mentioned anywhere in the local press.

So, from September 1901 to the present day, that area of Blackpool, which has seen development and change down the decades, has remained as the permanent home of Blackpool Football Club. It is known as Bloomfield Road, despite no official road actually existing at the time, and it has never changed its name. No sponsor to change its meaning and no vanity project from an owner who prefers to see their name emblazoned on the side of the structure. In fact, there have been times when even the name of Blackpool Football Club has been missing from the ground. As far back as the 1930s there wasn't a sign to signify that it was a football ground, and in recent years the intervention of supporters was the only thing that proved that the new ground actually played host to the local football club. It has been home for well over a century and has fought attempts to bring it down by a Manchester supermarket chain, and a well-meaning attempt to relocate the club to greenfield land on the edge of the M55. Bloomfield Road is Blackpool. It hopefully will not change.

The ground has changed though. From the ragtag selection of stands

that made it into the only four-sided ground in the country in 1906, to the rebuild after a serious fire to the West Stand in 1917. Four years later the ground had a capacity of 18,000, yet a home game against Bury was given as an attendance of 19,000. This was either a clerical error, or many men left that day significantly thinner than when they first arrived.

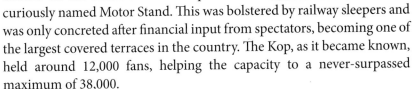

There was a Spion Kop that eventually made way for the modern South Stand, with all of its amenities, and the huge cinder terrace on the north side that replaced the curiously named Motor Stand. This was bolstered by railway sleepers and was only concreted after financial input from spectators, becoming one of the largest covered terraces in the country. The Kop, as it became known, held around 12,000 fans, helping the capacity to a never-surpassed maximum of 38,000.

There were the 'Scratching Sheds', or the East Paddock as the area was officially known, that gave no comfort whatsoever from the howling Irish Sea wind but did toy with the idea of seats for one season in the '70s. Such modern-day thinking was lost on the Blackpool fans at the time, and the idea was silently and quickly scrapped. In later years, as Bloomfield Road was being transformed, the temporary stand on the same spot was referred to as the 'Gene Kelly Stand' as the away fans would be singing in the rain due to the lack of a roof. The West Stand, blighted by smoke from the passing trains in the days of steam, was, at the end of its life, seemingly held together by will power alone, and the assorted corner stands that came and went just added to the lustre and uniqueness of Bloomfield Road. The rebuild of the stadium, which took longer than most cities after a war, finally achieved the seemingly unachievable. An all-seater stadium that looked soulless and disjointed with the 'temporary' East Stand replaced by another 'temporary' East Stand that continues to look totally out of place, despite its contribution to the intimidating atmosphere that the ground has become famous for. So, let us examine each side and take a look through the eyes of history.

The Kop in the 1950s. No roof and full of flat-capped supporters. And the West Stand with the 'curiously named' Motor Stand in its new home in the corner.

As the western side of the ground was the first to have the honour of a stand, then we will start there. That 300-seater stand remained in place for 17 years, a place for the directors and their wives to sit in comfort, although hampered by the presence of the press who had earlier pleaded with the club to invest a 'five-pound note' to build a press box. It was also hampered

by the wind blowing the steam and smoke from the railway sidings into the stand, but as they were the only ones sat in comfort, it was a small burden. The stand eventually burnt to the ground in 1917, the fire caused by a faulty heating system, and it destroyed not just the structure but the boardroom below, along with all the trophies (not that there were many) and club records. It made way for the extended West Stand that stood effectively unchanged for the next 80 years or so. For those who stood on it, whether you were watching Jimmy Hampson, Stanley Matthews, Alan Ball or Andy Garner, it was a challenge in itself. The terracing was narrow, so that any crowd of over ten people meant a constant bobbing of heads and craning of necks to see the action. The seats behind, which eventually held the directors and a small press box, were hard and wooden, and the proximity of the dugouts gave an insight into the tactical discussions during the game. They also gave a glimpse of the hopelessness of a cause when things were not going so well.

The press box was basically four rows of uncomfortable seating at the back of the stand, cordoned off from the fans by a three-sided concrete wall. I remember Jimmy Armfield suddenly calling for silence from the reporters at the end of the game as he was about to go live on 'national radio'. I was unimpressed by his haughty tone, until I saw him smile to himself as he put the microphone to his mouth. I recounted this to him years later. His reply was good old Jimmy: 'It worked, didn't it?'

Bloomfield Road in the '60s. Clearly before the decline as it is packed!

The press room under the stand, which had seen some of the most brilliant sports journalists and broadcasters (and me), was the size of a closet. It actually adjoined the far grander directors' room where Blackpool board members entertained their visiting counterparts, smiling through the brown fog of cigar smoke. The lesser mortals, who scribbled and jabbered into microphones, were fed pork pies and cups of tea. There was one particular radio broadcaster (whose name I will withhold) who used to sweep up most of the food and hide it in his jacket for the second half. He was the same man who missed a goal being scored while commentating. It was a windy and deserted night-time Bloomfield Road back in the '90s when Blackpool scored the opening goal. The equaliser came almost immediately and was greeted by virtual silence, as hardly any away fans had made the lengthy trip. The aforementioned commentator had actually dropped his pen and was scrabbling around looking for it when the goal went in. It took quite a few reassurances from his studio that the score was 1-1 and not 1-0 to Blackpool. Having said that, he was the man who gave me my media 'break', and a fine broadcaster.

Underneath the stand ran a walkway that was crammed at full time as fans left, some with transistor radios to their ears in the '70s, others with lighted cigarettes in their mouths in the '50s. Health & Safety was a long way from introducing itself, and it seemed only providence itself that saved the stand from catching alight from either the lit cigarettes or the screaming steam trains that passed by far too closely. The tracks served the Blackpool Central Station, which stood where the Coral Amusement Park stands today. It was at one stage the busiest train station in the world with 14 platforms, but it became a victim of Blackpool Council's interpretation of the Beeching cuts when they closed it down instead of the recommended North Station. For years afterwards the land stayed derelict and wasted, giving football hooligans of the '70s and '80s enough ammunition to keep them occupied. Now it is a car park, and the Yeadon Way that connects to the M55 follows the exact route of the train lines.

The current West Stand, now renamed the Sir Stanley Matthews Stand, is part of the three-sided structure that has transformed the ground. It is the main area of the stadium, replacing the South, and holds the reception area, hospitality suites, dressing rooms and offices. Its concrete structure and glass windows bear absolutely no resemblance whatsoever to the stand it replaced and was the first to be completed in the rebuild. In its short existence, it has seen more drama than most other areas of football grounds with protests and anger and despair. Only now does it feel like the peaceful haven of tranquility amid the madness of a matchday.

Of course, the defining image of Bloomfield Road throughout the years was the huge terrace at the north end of the ground, which inevitably became called 'The Kop', despite the original 'Spion Kop' being situated at the other end before the South Stand was built. It replaced the oddly named Motor Stand – which was moved to a position between the new terrace and the West Stand, showing that everything was worth saving at the club if it meant not having to spend any more money – and was opened in 1930 before the first game of the new season. Blackpool had reached the First Division for the first time, and this new cinder and timber terrace, stretching as far back as the eye could see, was packed with 12,000 heavily overcoated and tobacco ash-covered spectators. The occasion was so important that the Mayor had ceremoniously opened the stand with a rousing speech promising that Blackpool would be a 'force to be reckoned with' throughout the season, but in already predictable fashion, the team failed to live up to expectations and were soundly beaten 4-1 by a dominant Arsenal side before a record crowd of nearly 29,000.

The Kop remained effectively the same structure throughout its life, with the exception of it being concreted soon after its construction, until its sad demise at the end of the century. The only cosmetic changes included the addition of a roof that was taken down 20 years later in 1981 as the board decided it was too dangerous. It was later found that it would have been cheaper to repair, which added to the lengthening list of incomprehensible decisions made by whichever person was in charge at the time. Also, the two sides of the terrace became subject to segregation by huge metal fences following the murder of Kevin Olsson during the game with Bolton Wanderers in 1974.

Entering through the turnstiles at the back of the Kop and climbing the curious zig-zag steps to the top was an exciting experience, especially as the panoramic view from the highest position that was afforded was probably the best in the ground. From the 1930s until the 1960s this was a predominantly male experience, an escape from the ravages of pre- and post-war existences in many cases. The famous 'Atomic Boys' could be

found during the heady days of Matthews and Mortensen, the cries of 'Play up Jimmy' could be heard as Hampson ran down the centre and inevitably added to his goalscoring tally, and the first youthful chants emanated from the Kop as Ball, Armfield and Charnley fought the ever-growing threat of relegation. It was only in the 1970s that the Kop took on a new and sinister role.

The death of Kevin Olsson was a watershed in the history of spectating at English football grounds, although the measures quickly introduced were neither effective nor lasting. Walking up the familiar steps to the Kop was no longer exciting in the traditional sense but was now tinged with the expectation of misbehaviour and violence. Before the segregation fans were separated by a line of policemen, which was breached each time a goal was scored. Now there was a metal fence, but it didn't stop opposing fans mixing with each other or the consequences of such actions. Outside the ground there was a vast array of Black Maria police vans, waiting for the fans to spill out on to the wasteland that surrounded Bloomfield Road, a perfect environment for the hooliganism that was now overtaking and overwhelming the game. With the onset of easier travel through motorways and direct train lines, Blackpool became a magnet for travelling supporters, and so the Kop would be a seething mass of tangerine and whatever the colour of the opposing team, where the game was just a distraction. One solution was to house the entire away following on the Kop if it was too large to be policed, such as Manchester United and Aston Villa in the 1974-75 season. This was not popular amongst the Blackpool faithful, causing even more trouble.

By the time of the 1980s and 1990s, the team had fallen from grace and so the Kop was a bare shadow of its former self. Away followings were minimal, and by the time the club had created a new record in seeing riot police in an English football ground for the first time in history – against Birmingham City in 1989 – the Kop was off limits to Blackpool supporters as the west side was closed and derelict. The ground, always in need of a new last-minute safety certificate, was crumbling, and none more so than the famous north terrace. With the exception of a game with Colchester United in 1999, where an unusually generous gesture by the club allowed home fans on to the Kop, no Blackpool supporter had stood on the vast terrace for 15 years to support their team.

At the turn of the millennium, with the help of a football grant, the old West Stand and the Kop were demolished, the latter barely missed, and in its place rose the combined West and North Stands, the North now renamed The Stan Mortensen Stand. They were opened in February 2002, with Blackpool predictably losing 2-1 to Huddersfield Town, courtesy of an injury-time winner, just to prove that history continues to repeat itself.

The east side of the ground had a paddock there since virtually the beginning of the upgrade of the ground. It was one long terrace, made of concrete, that was eventually roofed in stages between 1926 and 1928, paid for by the supporters in what became a depressing regularity. Over the years it became known as the 'Scratching Sheds', although there is no real explanation as to why. There was a suggestion that when it was originally of cinder construction, the fans shuffling their feet gave the impression of scratching. That seemed rather unlikely, so the second explanation seems more believable in that it was effectively an overflow of the Kop, and as it was so busy in the 1920s, supporters were packed

The South Stand on the right. Bigger, better and far more comfortable than the other three.

together so tightly that they didn't have sufficient elbow room to scratch any part of their body, even if they had felt the need.

Whatever the reasons, the name certainly was apt for a stand that offered virtually no comfort whatsoever. The roof kept off the rain, but the shell of a stand that ran the full length of the pitch was inadequate to keep at bay the howling wind that normally accompanied a winter's game at Bloomfield Road. By the '60s and '70s it became a favourite spot for younger fans, who would sit on the concrete wall and put their legs between it and the wooden advertising hoarding in front, banging on the wood with their hands each time Blackpool attacked. At the rear of the stand there was a refreshment kiosk, which had stood seemingly since 1920, where two ladies served tea, dispensed from a huge urn, and cut ham and cheese sandwiches in half. The man walking the stand selling razor blades in the 1970s found his business surprisingly brisk, until the club authorities took a closer interest.

Below the stand were toilets that only the brave and seriously desperate would enter. These were unlit and seemingly untouched since their construction; the kind of amenities that might have been deemed inappropriate in the trenches. Running behind the stand was an alleyway at the back of Henry Street, which on busy matchdays would be a mass of humanity, but in the 1980s became a windswept wind tunnel where the empty carton boxes, newspapers and crisp packets accompanied the shivering spectators making their rapid journey home.

The stand did actually offer a modicum of comfort and modernity for one full season in the 1970s when seats were added to the terrace. This turned out to be a massive overestimation of a Blackpool fan's need for luxury, and it was a complete failure. The seats were dismantled after just 12 months.

The East Stand was demolished in the third stage of the rebuild of Bloomfield Road in 2003, to be replaced by a temporary open stand for away supporters only. Amusingly nicknamed 'the Gene Kelly Stand', as described earlier, it was replaced in turn by a larger covered stand for the start of the Premier League season; but of course was not ready in time, so the opening fixture was switched to Wigan Athletic's ground instead.

For many years up until segregation, the East Stand was where opposing supporters could mingle without fear of violence, and I can vividly remember being one of the boys sat on the concrete wall, my legs comfortably placed behind the advertising hoarding and chanting 'Blackpool' along with thousands of others in response to sky blue-scarved youngsters chanting 'City'. This was in 1971 against Manchester City in a 3-3 thriller. The same fixture on virtually the same date 28 years later saw the City fans housed exclusively in the Paddock, with those attending both fixtures noticing that it had hardly changed at all.

Blackpool
Football Club
Official Match Magazine

LEAGUE DIVISION FOUR

Saturday, 29th August, 1981
STOCKPORT COUNTY
Kick-off 3.0 p.m.
(PRICE 30p)

That brings us to the South Stand, the last to be redeveloped, but the one that was an iconic image of Blackpool Football Club throughout the years. Walking west along Bloomfield Road towards the South Stand ahead of a night fixture with the likes of Aston Villa, Wolves or Tottenham was one of the greatest pleasures of the old Bloomfield Road, the floodlights towering high and illuminating the surrounding area, the sense of expectation and anticipation and the smell of Bovril in the air. Once inside the South, its grandness and size seemed to dwarf all the others, despite the Kop being twice the capacity. To sit or even stand in the South felt like you were slightly richer, slightly cleverer and slightly more important than the rest. It was a stand that oozed character and personality, prestige and beauty, but is now completely lost in the identikit replacement.

It was built in 1925, replacing the old Spion Kop, and was hardly changed until its demolition nearly 80 years later. It held the reception, changing rooms, offices and boardroom that was furnished in the wood from the capsized HMS *Foudroyant* from Horatio Nelson's fleet, which sank off the Blackpool coast in 1897 (almost demanding a chapter in itself). The stand only initially held around 4,000, but most of them were in comfort previously unseen at the ground. Sitting in the seats above the terrace, you could watch as Hampson, Dodds, Matthews, Suddick, Bamber and Ellis ran on to the pitch from deep below, Joe Smith nonchalantly walking to the dugout or Billy Ayre racing to the edge of the area and screaming at the fans, his fists pumping and moustache bristling.

At the south-east of the stand was an uncovered corner overlooked by the 'Number 1' club. Every Saturday the roof of the club was full of men with pints in their hands watching the game unfold for free, but only imagining the action that was taking place in the three-quarters of the pitch they couldn't see.

In later years the South Stand was taken over by the younger fans, denied their rightful spot on the Kop, and so the chanting came predominantly from the southern end of the ground. At its beginning it was the preserve of the wealthier of the working-class men who came to Bloomfield Road once a fortnight, their flat caps keeping Brylcreemed hair in place. Long trench coats soon morphed into smart suits and thin ties, before Doc Martens and scarves tied at the wrist became the normal attire. Fashionable shell suits changed into replica shirts and the language became coarser and more demanding. All life's changes could be seen in the South Stand as a football club mirrored an ever-changing society.

Bloomfield Road has never been anywhere near a list of the greatest stadiums in the world, or even in Lancashire for that matter, but it has played host to an International fixture when England played Ireland in 1932. England won 1-0, courtesy of a Bobby Barclay goal, in front of approximately 25,000 fans. There have been numerous Football League representative matches played there, plus the women's UEFA Championship in 2005 saw three games at the half-completed stadium. Also, for reasons only known best by rugby league followers, Bloomfield Road has entertained the Northern Rail Cup on a regular basis.

The first live televised football match was at Bloomfield Road in 1960 when the 1000th Blackpool game to be played there was shown by ITV. The game was against Bolton Wanderers and Blackpool lost, of course. In the 1970s a TV camera point was built above the West Stand, which for the next 20 years managed to defy the elements for the likes of Gerald Sinstadt and John Motson to record Blackpool's slow and painful decline. Now the television cameras are housed in slightly more comfort, but up until recently still showed the temporary East Stand, which hardly did Bloomfield Road any favours.

Bloomfield Road. It is a name that is known, and we have now described the various structures that it was comprised of throughout the years, but what of the whole? How did it fit in with the age and the environment as the years passed by? It may be more than a football ground to many, but it was, and still is, a solid presence that has never moved. The surrounding area has changed, the attitudes to its presence have fluctuated and the people who flocked there, and also refused to enter, have their own connections.

For years the ground was deemed to be 'out of the way' and not really accessible. Those first few tentative seasons, when the fledgling club was trying to make its mark, saw it stranded amongst fields, hedgerows and a number of railway lines where steam engines would scream and splutter on their way to Central Station. The sparks that flew from the steel wheels would thankfully burn themselves out before igniting the wooden West Stand. When a railway line was disused, the sleepers would find their way to the Kop for the flat-capped supporters to stand on.

Gradually, the town of Blackpool physically embraced the football ground as people, factories and the inevitable boarding houses spread their arms and enveloped it. Blackpool blossomed as a town. The 'wakes week' became the focal point of a Lancashire family's year as the charabanc would bring holidaymakers to 'Blackpool-by-the-sea', and the population of 150,000 was outnumbered by the visitors of around eight million per year. The promenade and the Tower and the three piers and the Pleasure Beach complex were all vying for attention. The Winter Gardens, a stunning building that today has the grace of a fading visage, was the place for a night's entertainment. Blackpool was the best holiday destination in the country, and those who had the money and the desire stayed put and opened their own boarding houses and bed and breakfast establishments. This meant the ground was a passing distraction, but one that appealed on a Saturday afternoon, whether you supported Blackpool or not.

As the country came out of the post-war depression, the cleanliness of the sea air, compared to the soot-ingrained smog of the working-class towns, meant that more and more people dreamed of a 'nice little place in Blackpool'. Despite the success the club had in the 1950s, the ground stubbornly refused to enlarge, but the train lines were busier than ever, and the bus services ran 'specials' to Bloomfield Road on matchdays. At that time, the road was devoid of vehicles as men in long waterproof coats and trilbys walked shoulder-to-shoulder to the place of their adoration.

Once the attraction began to fade, so did the surrounding areas. The railway lines fell to the axe of Beeching, and left in their place was a barren wasteland, only separated from the ground by razor-topped barbed wire. The railway bridge that stood next to the Supporters' Club was too narrow for larger vehicles, and the corner newsagent stopped selling the matchday programme. By the 1980s the rugby league ground, hardly a passing distraction, was on the verge of saying goodbye, soon to be followed by the Mecca dancehalls. The nights of Northern Soul were at an end. The area around Bloomfield Road became a vandalised and graffiti-laden apocalyptic vision of the future, where Saturday afternoons were spent either battling with opposing fans if you were young and fearless, or trying to avoid the carnage if you were mature and sensible. Blackpool didn't have a football club. It didn't exist for the thousands of weekend revellers who drank, fought, loved and amused themselves in a town they hardly knew. Blackpool was the sin city of the UK, a place where every vice was embraced and the police's 'zero tolerance' was just a slogan. Bloomfield Road was ignored and the boarding houses put up their shutters whilst the poor population of the town struggled to get by on a measly wage, watching in despair as the promenade and its excesses imbibed more and more. Something was wrong. Blackpool was wrong.

The 'Las Vegas of England' never happened, but a transformation did

Where there once was a Kop, there is now an identikit stadium.

occur. As Bloomfield Road was being refurbished, rebuilt and redesigned, so the surrounding area followed suit. The country's 'biggest car park' took the place of the barren wasteland. Hotels were built, the boarding houses reopened with gleaming exteriors and the journey to the football ground was a civil affair. It had survived the threat of demolition when a supermarket chain came along, and it had survived the indignity of floodlights being lowered for safety reasons, terraces shut due to their state of disrepair, and safety certificates being granted on an annual basis. It had also survived the apathy of the local population, and then would have to survive the boycott – which it did. It still stands.

Whatever its failings, and the ground is certainly ready for some tender loving care, it is Blackpool's stadium and no one else's. Its bare, grey concrete façade that greets fans is not a thing of beauty, but there is no mistaking it once inside, with the tangerine seats and the words of Matthews, Mortensen and Armfield spelled out in white. It has seen so many dramas both on and off the pitch, and this being Blackpool FC, you can guarantee it will see many more. Only a future generation of supporters will read these words and look back with a knowing smile.

Before we leave this chapter, there should be a passing mention of the training ground…

'I was a lad when me dad took me to the training ground to watch the players. I remember it well. It was freezing and I had me hat and coat on, but me nose was red and me eyes were streaming with the wind. It didn't matter though cos I saw Matthews and Morty there, running around the pitch with all the others. They wore big thick grey jumpers and black shorts and ran in their football boots. You could see Stanley was fit. Me dad said that he ran on the beach every morning before breakfast, but

I just thought he was crazy. He wasn't crazy when he went on the pitch, though.

I kept going to the Squire's Gate every Monday morning as I didn't have to work that day. It was such a thrill at first, looking at the gleaming white huts and the immaculate green pitches. Even when the sun shone, it were still cold though. Every now and then a player would come over and say 'hello', and Ernie Taylor signed me autograph book.

It were only years later that I realised how shabby the place was. Alan Ball used to hate it there, even when he were manager. You could hear him screaming at his players. One of them told me that the only food they got was a big vat of porridge that the groundsman had made. Some of them would nip across to the café to get a bacon butty. Sometimes the water in the showers didn't work or it were cold. That's no way to treat footballers. A mate of mine said that 'if it were good enough for Matthews, it were good enough for this lot.' He was right, but this is the modern age.

The fence that separated me from the pitches was never mended. I could have walked right in if I wanted to. The huts were the same, but the rust on the doors meant they wouldn't close properly. They put a sign up to say it was Blackpool FC's training ground, but they spelt the word 'excellence' wrong. It were embarrassing.

One of the managers (I won't say who) said that he couldn't get players to come to the club because the training ground were so bad. Another player told me that new players weren't shown it until they'd signed a contract. Poor buggers.

Old Olly said it were a 'hellhole' and he'd just taken the team to the Premier League! I don't get it. Aren't the players the lifeblood of the team like the fans are of the club?

I don't go much now. It's too cold and by the time they build the new one they've been going on about for years, I'll be in me grave. What a club Blackpool is, eh?'

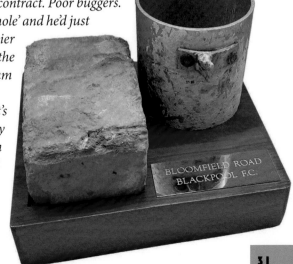

The Colours

Before we continue to look at the club's achievements and otherwise on the pitch, we should all remind ourselves that Blackpool Football Club is unique, and never more so than with the colour of their shirts. With the exception of Dundee United in Scotland, Blackpool are the only league club in the United Kingdom to play in tangerine. Not orange, but tangerine. It was orange for one season, 1923-24, when the colour was introduced by director Albert Hargreaves. He was an international referee who had taken charge of a Holland v Belgium game, and was so enthused with the orange colours that he immediately announced that Blackpool would play in them the following season. At the time they were playing in white shirts and blue shorts, but then club colours meant very little.

The number of different kits and colours that Blackpool wore in the early days was like a kaleidoscope of paint thrown randomly in the hope that the most vibrant would stick. Red shirts, white shirts, blue shirts, striped shirts, sky blue shirts and even red, yellow and black shirts in deference to Belgian refugees during the First World War. The orange stayed briefly, but it was

1915   1919   1923   1935

accompanied by black shorts and collars, which made the whole effect rather dazzling and disorientating. It was scrapped apparently after the players said they had struggled to see each other during a particularly foggy cup game at Blackburn and so, within 12 months, the unusual combination of dark and light blue stripes became the official kit. No one knows why. Thankfully, by the time of the 1938/39 season, the shirts had taken on a slightly lighter hue of orange and became officially tangerine. It has not changed since. Today the colours of a club almost define its existence. Could anyone now imagine Manchester United in anything other than red? Well, they played against Blackpool in the 1948 FA Cup final in blue, and in the 1968 European Cup final, too. Blackpool is tangerine, though. It is inexplicable that any other colour should be associated with the club, but they played that 1948 final in white shirts and again in 2010 in the Championship Play-off final. Thankfully on that occasion the tangerine shorts were used as an official second kit, but in 1948 they wore blue shorts. Not a smidgeon of tangerine to be seen anywhere.

GUESS WHICH CLUB

Just a few of Blackpool FC's rainbow historical colour schemes – before they were all eclipsed by tangerine.

The away colours have always been a thing of the moment. Traditionally, Blackpool have just swapped the shirts and shorts colours, but in the more recent commercial age, new and unusual combinations have been found. A recent blue-striped kit is a throwback to the 1930s but, in my opinion, it doesn't say Blackpool FC. What does say Blackpool FC is the colour tangerine.

The home shirts have stayed effectively the same since 1938, albeit with the arrival of gaudy sponsors (of which 'Rebecca's' was probably the low point), sometimes tinged with white and a small splash of blue. There was one memorable occasion when the Latvian colours of mauve were used as a tribute to the new investor Valeri Belokon, but thankfully that was for only one game. For a few seasons, the whole ensemble was tangerine with white shorts being abandoned, and in one unforgettable season (1989-90) the club attempted to follow the Dutch national side's lead by introducing

a diamond pattern on the shirt. This turned the tangerine to salmon pink and was quickly scrapped, along with the manager and most of the players as relegation had returned to its occasional home of Blackpool. No, tangerine is Blackpool's colour and it lit up the Premier League for one crazy season – and despite Prince Philip saying rather unkind things about it before the 1953 FA Cup final, it will always be Blackpool's colour.

The colour of a team's shirt is now a defining characteristic of the club, but for the first 30 years or so of the professional game, it really didn't matter. Now a fan will go to a game wearing a replica shirt with his hero's name printed on the back. Some will carry flags, some will wear lucky underwear in their team's colours, some will wear baseball hats. Yet when football first became a popular sport, spectators were uniformly grey, predominantly men with long coats and caps and hats and no indication as to who they were supporting. Having said that, very few people travelled to an away game before the Second World War. Normally, a goal was celebrated by waving white handkerchiefs in the air, or in the more extravagant areas, caps were thrown with gusto. This didn't seem to happen at Blackpool.

The first evidence of Blackpool 'colours' being worn was at Wembley in 1948 when tangerine rosettes were part of the dress code, along with the occasional knitted scarf in 'near enough' colours to keep the wind at bay. It was only after 'The Atomic Boys' came on the scene (more of them later) that the vivacious and eye-catching tangerine started to appear as blazes of sunshine amid the grey demeanour of the terraces. Scarves, bobble hats, badges. That is where it started. Isn't it good that Blackpool play in such a startling colour? How else would you have recognised the Blackpool supporter at a foggy and misty Ewood Park? Tangerine is Blackpool. Blackpool is tangerine.

The Managers

Up to the time of writing, Blackpool Football Club has had 38 full-time managers. Some of them were spectacularly successful, some failing from day one. Some stayed far longer than was naturally expected, whilst others seem to depart almost before they sat behind the desk. The old joke of chalking the manager's names on the office door, so as to save paint, was probably told at Bloomfield Road first.

For longevity, no one gets close to Joe Smith. His 23-year reign is a lifetime, and not likely to be repeated in modern football, and especially at Blackpool. A former player for Bolton Wanderers, who appeared in the famous 1923 FA Cup final and scored an astonishing 277 League and cup goals for The Trotters – only eight behind Nat Lofthouse – he arrived at Blackpool via a four-year stint with Reading, and an earlier two-year player-manager role at Darwen. At the time, the Seasiders were a struggling Second Division side, but in his second season they were promoted back to the top flight.

A stocky man, immaculately dressed in a three-piece suit, Smith used to walk to the ground from his home each morning, and was regarded as a father figure and motivator as opposed to a tactician. Hardly a screamer from the touchline (at a time when that kind of thing would probably have been frowned upon), he always seemed to have a quiet word of encouragement or a louder word of lambast, depending on how the game was going. A joker in the dressing room, an eye for a talented player and a shrewd business mind, and the seeds were sown for the most successful manager the club has had.

The statistics don't really tell the story. Three FA Cup finals, one victory. A runners-up spot in the First Division and promotion from the Second. That's it. In 23 years, that was the achievement, but what the stats don't reflect are the levels of performance that the Blackpool side produced from 1939 until his departure. This was a team that could quite easily have won the title in the 1939-40 season, if World War II hadn't happened. Admittedly, this is one of the least important facts in the history of that terrible conflict, and it's not my intention to belittle it, but it's true that Blackpool had a team that was regarded as the best in the country.

During the war years, with football played mainly to keep up morale, Blackpool were a real attraction. Players such as Matthews and Dodds embraced invitations to play for the club, and the 1943 War Cup final against Arsenal – whose side had been photographed with the trophy *before* the match – was testament to the talent he spotted and nurtured. Blackpool's 4-2 victory from two down was regarded as justice for a side that just played football in the most entertaining manner.

After the war, they became one of the best. The famous 'M' forward line of Matthews, Mortensen and Mudie was all of Smith's doing. The 1948 FA Cup final, regarded as the greatest footballing final of all time, was again made possible by him. 'The Matthews Final' was him. The battle for the title, finishing an eventual distant second to the powerhouse that had become Manchester United, was him. He was Blackpool Football Club, and they owed everything to him in those heady days when the tangerine shirts lit up the gloom in a pre-floodlight era.

His departure in 1958 was sad. The official reason was that old age and health had forced his retirement, yet that was

not true. He was sacked after refusing to resign. On 1st February 1958 he was sent his dismissal notice after he had left home with the team for a game at Aston Villa. He saw out his last three months and left football at the end of the season. As he said in a newspaper interview with the *Daily Mirror*, 'After fifty years in the game, I wanted to go out the clean way. I don't call this the clean way.'

The club did give him a golden handshake though, gave him a rent-free house and paid him a lifetime pension, but it seems as tacky as the souvenir shops that make up the promenade. His stature was, and still is, great. I unashamedly take an excerpt from an interview with Stanley Matthews for *Blackpool Football,* the history written by Robin Daniels in 1972.

'Joe was a canny manager. He had a personality about him. Joe was a comedian. He could tell the same joke twenty times every day, and you'd laugh every time... he didn't hold many tactical talks. He would say a few words before the match. He just wanted players to keep their individuality and he achieved good team-work.'

To stay as manager for such a long time, with the team consistently in the First Division despite some of the lowest attendances in the top flight, was an achievement that stands alongside the likes of Sir Alex Ferguson and Bill Shankly. It is unlikely to be repeated.

Nobody comes close to Smith's 23-year tenure, with only Ron Suart and Sam Ellis lasting beyond expectancy with nine and seven years, respectively. Suart was one of the club's former players who returned as a manager but had the unenviable job of stepping into Joe Smith's shoes. He had played over 100 times as a full-back for Blackpool, sadly missing the 1948 FA Cup Final through injury, and he returned to Bloomfield Road full of enthusiasm and vigour. In his first season, 1958-59, the team finished in the top ten, continuing an expectancy that the Tangerines would always be there, but that was the last time it ever happened. For Suart, quietly spoken, dignified, hard-working, the job was a struggle. Despite discovering new talents such as Alan Ball and Ray Charnley, the abolition of the maximum wage and the gradual decline of the club meant that the trapdoor to the Second Division was opening wider each year. When the club finally fell through it in 1967, Suart resigned, following numerous requests for him to leave by a jittery board. He left with his head held high, however, and found further employment at Chelsea.

Sam Ellis could be mistaken for Major Buckley, Blackpool's second full-time manager, in that his style was down-to-earth and blunt. A no-nonsense defender with Sheffield Wednesday, he arrived at a decrepit and depressing Bloomfield Road with the team firmly in the Fourth Division and attendances at their lowest since the turn of the century. He had no management experience and had to face the ignominy of re-election in his first season in charge. Even though Blackpool had finished fourth bottom of the Fourth Division and just about every other club voted for them to remain in the Football League, the fact that they were there at all was an embarrassment in itself. When a low is reached and there really is nowhere else to go, then it takes a strong and determined person to reinvigorate and enthuse. That is what Ellis did, and with shrewd loans (as there was virtually nothing in the bank for players) he turned the team's fortunes around and managed to get Blackpool promoted at the third time of asking. Any fan amongst the 3,000 that travelled to Darlington on that Mayday Wednesday evening will remember the passion, the dominance and the celebrations. Ellis had tapped into something. The future was tangerine at a time when the marketing slogan hadn't even been devised, never mind stolen, but that's where the juggernaut of success came to a shuddering halt. Third Division football was bigger and better, and Blackpool struggled again. Ellis was sacked. Aren't they all?

Suart had been the first former player to return as manager; the second was Stan Mortensen. It's hard to understand now, some 50 years after the events when so many bad decisions have been taken in what is a constant rerunning of history, but the shabbiness that 'Morty' experienced was beyond anything seen at the club before. Sadly, it is now a constant theme.

Stan Mortensen was of course one of the greatest players in Blackpool FC's history, so when he was approached to replace Ron Suart, it was greeted with unbridled enthusiasm from just about every fan who wore a tangerine scarf. He couldn't save the club from relegation in 1967, as the team's underwhelming performances had secured a backstep in the football pyramid, but within 12 months he had transformed the attitude and the very ethos of the club. With the signing of a young firebrand (on the field at least) from Scotland in Tony Green, and a marked attacking style, they were set for promotion at the first attempt. It was a given. It was a fairy tale. It didn't happen.

It's difficult to believe how unlucky Blackpool were on that final day of the season. Six consecutive victories, 4,000 Pool fans on a soaking wet Saturday in Huddersfield, and a second-half performance that brought a 3-1 win. They were promoted... but they weren't. As the fans chanted and celebrated, the whispers ran through the crowd like a swarm of insects, the buzzing and the insistence increasing with every retelling. In the pre-internet days, only those who had transistor radios were kings, and their message was damning. An Aston Villa own-goal in injury time had given QPR a 2-1 victory and the second place for promotion. Blackpool missed out by .21 of a goal, when goal average was used. Those who were mathematical geniuses on the Leeds Road pitch were kept busy.

The immortal Morty – from goalbanger to pen-pusher.

Morty kept smiling. It was his way. Do it next season instead, but the next season was a dampener with a poor League finish, despite the arrival of more Scottish talent, notably Tommy Hutchison. The next season, he was sacked. Aren't they all?

Blackpool FC has a rather disturbing habit of making inexplicably bad decisions, and that was one of the first in the modern era. Mortensen didn't complain. He didn't point fingers and he didn't seek compensation. He kept on supporting the club and the town and stayed until the end of his life. A truer legend has never been seen at Bloomfield Road.

Others who returned as manager after playing for the club were Allan Brown and Alan Ball, the former who had two spells with the club, and the latter whose stay can only possibly be described as 'catastrophic'. Brown had taken the team to the edge of the promotion race in 1978 after

two home games that had brought two victories and ten goals. He was sacked. It came after a disagreement with the board that was never made public. Cue the word 'inexplicable' again. He did return later for a brief spell whilst the team languished in the Third Division but walked out just as quickly.

Ball was another fairy-tale appointment. How could he fail? One of the most exciting players of his generation, who still had a bond with his first club as a professional, but the less said about his tenure then probably the better. Of course, the human trait is to look for the bad and the failure as opposed to the good and the successful, so in Alan Ball it was all there. The now-famous video clip of him screaming at two bemused young players on the training pitch who were incapable of doing what came naturally to him. The open criticism of the Blackpool fans who were accused of wanting their side to lose in an FA Cup tie with non-league neighbours Fleetwood Town, and the inexorable slide down the table as virtually every result went against them. Ball was sacked. Wasn't it inevitable?

Two-term managers all seemed to share the same experience. Returning was like reuniting with a true love after a bitter split-up. It could never be the same, and so it was for Allan Brown, Bob Stokoe and Simon Grayson.

Stokoe had brought almost immediate success to the club after his appointment. Despite arriving too late to save the team from relegation from the First Division in 1971, and his lukewarm approach to a summer tournament called the Anglo-Italian Cup, his team won it – so giving

Blackpool their first silverware since 1953.

'Let's have a break from football. I'll do what sorting out has to be done with the playing staff. Then we'll get down to pre-season training.'

Those words were spoken before the tournament started, but there is nothing like winning, and holding a trophy aloft gave him and the players all the confidence they needed. Unfortunately, the promotion push didn't immediately materialise, and despite his public proclamation that he wanted to stay at Blackpool for 'at least five years', he resigned and joined Sunderland in 1973. The familiar and famous image of Stokoe running half the length of the pitch to embrace Jim Montgomery at the end of the 1973 FA Cup final at Wembley was lost on all Leeds United and Blackpool fans. Stokoe returned a few years later with the club sliding down the greasy pole of despair, and like Brown, he left quickly.

Stokoe was loved by his players, though. Peter Suddaby, who played 370 times for the club, regarded him as someone special:

'He always showed great trust in me, especially after I made three crucial

errors in my first three matches. Each time he called me into his office on the Monday and told me I was playing in the next match, but I needed to learn from my mistakes. Not many managers would do that.'

Simon Grayson was brought into the club as a player-manager after the long, drawn-out departure of Colin Hendry. He so impressed owner Owen Oyston that he made the position permanent – and the rest, as they say, is history. Well, his first tenure, anyway. In his first full season he had taken Blackpool back to the Championship for the first time in 29 years. The 'perfect ten' at the end of the season perfectly encapsulated everything that was about his style of play. It was entertaining and daring, stylish and solid at the same time. The Play-off final against Yeovil Town at Wembley was one of the most one-sided in the history of the competition, and Grayson's legend at Blackpool was secure.

Following 'consolidation' seasons in the higher division and a slowing down of the high-tempo football, the team stagnated, and Grayson was lured to his real love, Leeds United. His success there, at Huddersfield Town and with rivals Preston North End (never likely to endear him to the Blackpool faithful again) gave him the title of the 'League One

King'. All four clubs he had managed had been promoted to the Championship. The record soon faltered and disappointments at Bradford City and, spectacularly, Sunderland (in full view of documentary TV cameras) sullied his once-untouchable reputation – and so it was a surprise when new Blackpool owner Simon Sadler called him back after the rather unsettling departure of Terry McPhillips.

A hero in December and sacked in February, Grayson was much the victim of the new social-media 'death-by-a-thousand-cuts' as each defeat saw more abuse, professional and personal, heaped on by an unforgiving fanbase.

His sacking came just seven months after he had been offered a three-year contract and had overseen a remarkable 12 new playing additions during the transfer window. If ever a manager was sacked by the fans…

Certain managers arrive and leave without leaving any footprint whatsoever, and some arrive and leave before the seat in the manager's office even gets warm. The shortest stay was achieved by Michael Appleton, who after protracted contract negotiations with his current club Portsmouth, agreed to take over from Ian Holloway – but after just 65 days he resigned and joined Blackburn Rovers, only to be sacked 67 days later. He took over the record from Graham Carr, who lasted just four months in 1990, although his dismissal did at least bring about the Billy Ayre era.

Billy Ayre, Crocodile Dundee and a refugee from the Planet of the Apes.

Other notable one-term managers were Jimmy Mullen (who seemed to have a permanent smile), Les Shannon (who at least managed to get Blackpool back into the First Division), Stan Ternant (who didn't really enjoy his time at Bloomfield Road), Gary Megson (who really didn't seem to enjoy himself at all), Jose Riga (the only foreign coach to be employed), Neil McFarland and Lee Clarke. In fact, the average tenure of a Blackpool manager or coach since 1990 is just 18 months. Not exactly a secure position.

Some managers were despised and almost hated, others almost universally adored. In the former category could be placed Colin Hendry, Nigel Worthington, Sam Allardyce and maybe even Steve McMahon, although he could also appear in the next category depending on his relationship with the fans. Those who were loved, as well as the obvious Smith and Mortensen, were Billy Ayre and Ian Holloway. Both of these managers are discussed in the most reverential tones by Blackpool supporters.

Ayre was a fist-pumping, screaming firebrand who ran on to the pitch and dared the fans not to make a noise. His force of personality transformed a relegation-haunted team into promotion contenders within a few short months. He made Bloomfield Road a fortress, creating a record of 12 months without a defeat at the ground, winning 15 League games in succession; yet away from home there was a fragility. The Blackpool team he created saw despair in the Play-off final on a bitterly cold Friday night as Torquay United stood up to a penalty shoot-out better than Blackpool. His famous comment about 'never having a worse moment in my life, never mind football' was spoken as the floodlights were turned off and the majority of the fans were making their long way home. A year later, on a sunny Saturday, his team triumphed, but it needed penalties again.

The away fragility was never clearer than at a game at rivals Burnley, where 6,000 travelling fans helped Turf Moor to see a 21,000 crowd in a top-of-the-table Fourth Division encounter on a Tuesday evening. Predictably, Blackpool lost 2-0, and when he was asked by a radio reporter after the game about the passion from the players, he responded in downcast fashion that he'd 'seen more passion on a park bench on a Sunday morning', which summed up his brusque personality – something the author saw first-hand on numerous occasions.

It was the Bloomfield Road experience that made Billy Ayre the legend he became. Sacked of course by Owen Oyston after four years, two of them struggling in the higher division with a weaker squad than the one he'd achieved promotion with; his name rang around the ground during a League Cup game the following season as new manager Sam Allardyce looked on in bemusement. A few years later, not long before his untimely death, he was spotted amongst the Blackpool crowd at the Millennium Stadium as Blackpool were playing in the final of the Football League Trophy. He was carried shoulder high by the supporters who had taken him to their hearts, and who still talk of him in adoring tones. Billy Ayre was, and still is, a Blackpool legend.

What do you say about Ian Holloway that hasn't already been said? Taking a 'career break' from the game after a disastrous relegation with Leicester City, he suddenly became the new Blackpool manager in 2009. There are so many stories of how and why this came about, notably the (maybe apocryphal) one of him forcing Chairman Karl Oyston to interview him; but it was a straight fight between himself and Iain Dowie, and he won. What followed was, of course, history. A team that had no right to achieve, according to expert opinion, but one that produced some of the most wild and breathless football ever seen at Bloomfield Road. The second half at Nottingham Forest's City Ground in the Play-off semi-final second leg was possibly the greatest 45 minutes of football ever played by a Blackpool team. This was a season where they beat their promotion rivals four times and inflicted home defeats on them twice after an unending run of victories. The first half of the Play-off final at Wembley was probably the craziest ever seen at the stadium, but it was all Holloway's doing. His belief was that the only way to attack the

Ollie hits the back of the net.

Premier League was to do just that, to attack, and it led to a season that stretched nerves to breaking point and gave the ecstasy of football a new level. He played on the 'little Blackpool' tag and it worked as the David slew Goliath on a regular weekly basis. How Blackpool failed to avoid relegation that season is still one of those conspiracy-theory moments.

Even after the dismantling of the Premier League side, he somehow replaced the Adam, Vaughan, Campbell (and others) combination with Ferguson and Phillips and got to Wembley again. This time it was all about West Ham, though. Two years before it had been Blackpool who were the darlings, but now the crisis that was the east London club was all that mattered, and a poor refereeing performance and sloppy finishing meant that Holloway's tenure was ending quickly. Having created a masterpiece at the beginning of the next season, only to see it revealed as a paint-by-numbers picture, he departed for the giants of English football, Crystal Palace. This was not lost on the unforgiving fans who always expected a move to take over at Liverpool or Manchester United or Barcelona. His friendship with the Oyston family did not endear him, and now he isn't regarded anywhere near as highly as he should be as he takes his managerial career further and further down the footballing pyramid.

There are so many other managers that I haven't referred to, so for the record here they are. Tom Barcroft, Jack Cox, Bill Norman, Sydney Beaumont, Harry Evans, Sandy MacFarlane, Jimmy Meadows, Harry Potts, Paul Ince, Barry Ferguson, Lee Clarke, Gary Bowyer and the current incumbent (at the time of writing), Neil Critchley. The earlier managers are now relatively forgotten, sadly, but in recent years the likes of Potts and Worthington went on to better things (as did Mullen and Allardyce, who is the only England manager with a 100 per cent win record, albeit after only one game), while Ince and Clarke were universally despised. Bowyer was the 'one that got away' and Critchley is the man who is now expected to lead the club to a better future. Only time will tell.

GALLAHER'S CIGARETTES.

JOHN COX,
BLACKPOOL. 1909-10.

Being a football manager is an enterprise every bit as safe and stable as walking a cliff edge, trying to guess where the solid land ends and the empty space starts. Being a Blackpool manager must sometimes feel like you are walking the same crumbling path, only blindfolded. Decisions taken by the board of directors or the owners have been difficult to explain, as in the case of Joe Smith. Stan Mortensen's sacking is still a cloud hanging above Bloomfield Road even after 50-odd years, as is the inexplicable dismissal of Billy Ayre a quarter of a century later. Add that to Allan Brown's untimely departure and the almost comic-book farewells of Steve McMahon and Jose Riga and it is fair to say that the revolving door is still in use. McMahon's eventual departure

was expected after a predictable falling-out with the owner and the fans, whilst the farewell to Riga was ridiculous. In a job, out of a job and then in one again, before he decided that enough was enough. Both managers make a reappearance later in the book, but all Blackpool fans will have their own memories of those 'special' times. Every football manager seems to get the sack eventually, and nearly every Blackpool manager experiences it.

On a final note, when I was researching this book, I asked on social media which manager Blackpool fans regarded as the greatest manager. Maybe I didn't ask the right question, but all but one said Ian Holloway. Joe Smith only received one vote, yet he was the man who transformed a small, sleepy football club into the powerhouse they became during the 1950s. Memories are short, and never more so than with football fans.

A s each manager sits down in the well-worn seat behind the mahogany desk, the bare walls staring back and the inadequate heater battling the cold, they ask similar questions.

How do I stop the boy Doherty from leaving?

Why isn't Jimmy scoring any more?

Is Stan going to be fit?

How do I keep this lot in the First Division?

How do I get Suddick to do more?

Where will we train today?

Why aren't we flying there? We're Premier League, aren't we?

Can I get this man on loan before the boss finds out?

Is this real?

Am I getting the sack?

The manager's office has seen and heard it all. It will see and hear it again.

The Players

This is the difficult part. During the lifespan of Blackpool Football Club, it is estimated that around 1,500 different players have pulled on the jersey (of whichever colour it was at the time) to play for the team. So, who to choose? Listing them all would be an endeavour of mammoth proportions. Listing a few would almost certainly leave out a favourite. Listing none would be like going to the cinema and staring at a blank screen. Could it be done decade by decade? Yes, but whereas the 1950s could have a complete book by itself, the 1980s may barely be worthy of a sentence. Instead, I have decided to mention the influential players, the ones who were instrumental in the success of a particular Blackpool team at that time. It is a virtually impossible task, and I can guarantee your 'hero' will not be amongst them.

It is not possible to mention Blackpool Football Club's history and not have Sir Stanley Matthews in the same sentence. It is also virtually impossible to add anything new about a player who would easily have stood among the giants of the game, no matter which decade he played in. If you think of Messi and Ronaldo today, he would have been there. If you think of Beckham and Zidane, he would have been there. If you think of Maradona and Pele, he would have been there. If you think of Puskas and... well, he was there, and he was the greatest.

FOOTBALLERS
(A Series of 50)
Photos by courtesy of
Buchan Publications

No. 20

STAN MATTHEWS
(Blackpool)

What is there first to be said about the maestro of football? Probably the greatest outside-right ever. Known throughout the world as the Wizard of Dribble, but more important is a real example to youngsters. Never guilty of a foul and a real sportsman.

DICKSON ORDE & CO. LTD.
Farnham : Surrey

I never saw him play. Few here reading this have. I met him once, and he was the most unassuming famous person I had ever experienced. In a time before the obligatory 'selfie', he patiently signed autographs and listened to the same retelling of stories over and over again, with a smile and kind word. He agreed to be at my first book signing back in 1992, not knowing who I was and actually not getting paid that much. Nothing was too much trouble for him, yet this was a man who had taken the game in the 1950s to a new and extraordinary level. In a team that was one of the most powerful in the country, it was said that his name on the sheet would add thousands to an attendance. Looking at the figures for the day, I am sure that is totally correct.

He played 440 times for the club. He played for 33 years, longer than any other at that level. His England career lasted longer than anyone else's. His fitness was at a level that only the modern-day footballer can aspire to. At a time when players would smoke a cigarette and take a quick run up and down the pitch, he would fast, take a sip of tea, employ the most eye-watering stretching exercises and use the seven golden miles of sand as his own personal gymnasium. Is it any wonder that when he left the club to continue his career back at Stoke City at the age of 46, he was still able to produce performances that baffled opposing defenders?

We have all seen the grainy black-and-white films and images of the famous body swerve, where he shimmies to the left whilst the ball inexplicably goes to the right. We all know the story of the 1953 FA Cup final which is forever immortalised as 'The Matthews Final', despite Mortensen scoring a hat-trick (we will return to this later), and we all know that he was the first winner of the Ballon d'Or in 1956 (rather surprisingly, the only Blackpool player to have been voted the best in the world up to now). We know that he was the first footballer to receive a knighthood. There is nothing new to add to this incredible story. He was one of the greatest footballers to walk the planet, and he played for Blackpool.

He played for the club from 1941 as a guest (his first appearance was against Preston North End in a 1-0 defeat) but didn't sign officially until 10th May 1947, when Joe Smith paid £11,500 for the 32-year-old. By the way, just think about that. £11,500 was an extraordinary amount of money back then, yet the club happily paid it for a player who was past 30 years of age! He already lived in Blackpool, where he owned a hotel, and the lure of the seaside was too great for the man from Stoke.

Once the ink had dried (and Joe Smith had chortled all the way back to his office), Matthews then appeared for the club right through the glory years until 1961, winning the famous FA Cup winners' medal (which meant so much more in those days) and appearing in two other finals. He was Blackpool. If people talked of Blackpool FC, they talked of Stanley Matthews. He wore the tangerine shirt brighter and with more commitment than most any other player. He was simply the best player the club had ever seen and has ever seen since. Even before he became a fully-fledged Blackpool player, he created sporting headlines with his astonishing performance in the 1943 War Cup final against an arrogant Arsenal side who had taken a team photograph with the trophy before the game. Blackpool came from two goals behind to win it 4-2, and it was Matthews who made it happen.

He rarely scored, but the 1952-53 season saw him in prolific form with four goals. One of them was in the 8-4 home victory over Charlton

Athletic which resulted in calls for his return to the England squad, after being overlooked. He was 37 at the time. Just as an aside and to prove that all Blackpool fans are paranoid and absolutely convinced that everything conspires against them, I saw the *Sunday Pictorial* headline after that hammering which said 'CHARLTON, 8-1 DOWN, GO ON FIGHTING' – just about the most bizarre reading of a one-sided game in history. Today it would cause uproar and petitions being signed on social media.

When fans attended a Blackpool game, the first name they would look for on the team sheet printed in the programme was Matthews. This was at a time when the programme was about the most accurate guide to the day. If Stanley was there, then Blackpool had more than just a fighting chance, but if he wasn't…

The 'bright lights' of London didn't appeal (as was the case with other players who made their name at the club and decided it was for life), but he always seemed to have his best games down there. After a particularly impressive match against Arsenal, a *Times* correspondent wrote:

'Highbury is champagne to him. The bubbles tickle his toes, the old magic flows out, the heroic actor in a favourite theatre, holding an entranced worshipping public in the palm of his hand.'

The newspapers weren't always so kind, though. One of the reasons for Matthews' inconsistent appearances for England was the smear campaign aimed at him at times, but it's difficult to imagine the impact this man had on the game. For those brought up on Beckham and Rooney, then it's similar, but frankly in a different league. Matthews was known the world over in a pre-internet age where word-of-mouth and radio commentaries were the social media of the day. Blackpool were invited to play all over the world in lucrative friendly tournaments, not because of the club but because of the man. The Sierra Leone club, Socro United, changed their name to The

Mighty Blackpool in 1954 because of Matthews, and in Canada he was referred to as 'Mr Football' when he was reported on. Can you imagine any Blackpool player, before and since, having such an impact all over the world, never mind at Bloomfield Road?

After he left and returned to Stoke City, there was a void. It was inconceivable that a Blackpool team would run out on to the pitch and there wasn't a Stanley Matthews stretching and jumping up and down on the spot, with a quiet encouraging word to a younger player or a knowing look with Stan Mortensen. The era had ended, and with it the decline of the team's fortunes continued apace. This interview is taken from Robin Daniels' history of the club in 1972 and gives a measure of Matthews, the man and footballer.

'If you're in a team and you're playing well, playing good football, and you lose – that is no good. You've got to win; there is no doubt about it. Entertainment must come second. Supporters say, 'Oh, what a terrible game – but they've won.' It is better to play badly and win, than to play well and lose.

I love the game. I love football and I wanted to play as long as I could. I played in first-class football until I was fifty. I knew very well that I had the stamina… My mental outlook was: 'I KNOW I can do it'

I go back to Bloomfield Road now and then, but I don't want them to go to the trouble of providing a special ticket for me. I like to slip in at the back so that no-one will notice.'

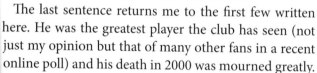

The last sentence returns me to the first few written here. He was the greatest player the club has seen (not just my opinion but that of many other fans in a recent online poll) and his death in 2000 was mourned greatly.

It is almost impossible to mention Matthews and not mention Mortensen in the same breath. The two Stanleys. One fleet of foot, the other a powerhouse with a thunderbolt shot. If Matthews was regarded as the greatest player to have worn a tangerine shirt, then Morty was the best 'Blackpool player' ever. There is a distinction. The two played together as part of the famous 'M' forward line (Mudie being an integral part) and they towered over jittery defences as Blackpool threatened to conquer

English football. The fact that the only trophy in their years together at club level was an FA Cup final victory (no matter how important that was) speaks volumes on the uncertainty of success and failure. Blackpool were the best team in the country but couldn't prove it.

Morty was a phenomenon. He scored 222 goals for the club and 23 for England at a rate of virtually a goal a game for his country. Of course, he scored the hat-trick in 1953 and then good-naturedly smiled when the game was renamed 'The Matthews Final', despite the maestro only really playing well for the last 20 minutes. To this day, no other player has managed to score three goals in English football's showpiece occasion. In those days, when football was the preserve of the working-class men who crowded on the terraces, or the families huddled together around the wireless set, players such as Mortensen were just a name, a player, but not a personality. Even the first live television coverage in 1953 didn't 'personalise' the man, but what couldn't be confused was the sheer power that was unleashed when Morty scored the free-kick with two minutes to go, to level against Bolton Wanderers. The legendary Ernie Taylor had said that 'there's no gap', but Morty saw one. That would be enough, especially as just 60 seconds later Bill Perry would get the winner after another moment of Matthews' trickery on the right. Instead, there's a different story, told by the man himself.

'The true interpretation is that a gypsy on the Golden Mile that year had said that Blackpool were going to win the Cup, and as I ran to the ball, I thought that she cast a spell over the arena and picked the ball up and threw it into the net, and then brought everyone back to life, and I got the credit for it.'

No one in the stadium, or in their living rooms listening on the radio or squinting at the impossible-to-see television images knew of the gypsy. She scored the goal, not Morty, so really he wasn't the only player to score a Cup final hat-trick. In a way, the story sums up the man. Never being given enough credit for Blackpool's only major success in their history, he chose to make light of it instead of screaming and shaking with anger. One can only imagine what would happen today in this social-media world we inhabit.

There is the well-known story of the England game when Tom Finney had been drafted in to replace Matthews and had supplied two crosses for Morty to head in. On both occasions, Stan held his head in some distress. When Finney asked him what was wrong, he replied, 'Thanks for your good work Tom, but you see Stanley centres the ball so that the lace points away from me.'

Morty scored goals because that was what he was made to do. He scored a hat-trick in the 1948 FA Cup semi-final and then scored against Manchester United in the final, meaning he managed to score a goal in every round of the competition that season. He was Blackpool's top scorer for eleven consecutive seasons, from his first to his last at the club. Only Allan Brown came close in one campaign. He was 'Mr Blackpool' and when he was transferred to Hull City in late 1955, the town was collectively in a state of shock. Today he has a statue in his honour outside the ground which, with the exception of one infamously shabby moment, has stood in its glory daring the younger fans to ask their peers who he was. He was 'Mister Blackpool'.

'To me, the name Blackpool Football Club is the most important thing in the world. We're part of a wonderful organisation, and I say to my players time after time: "Whenever you're playing away from home, wherever you are, you're looked upon as ambassadors of Blackpool Football Club." ...At all times I place Blackpool Football Club right at the top.'

Those words were spoken in an interview when he was manager, not long before his badly handled dismissal. Thankfully, his legend wasn't tarnished to any degree, as was proven when hundreds lined the streets of the town at his funeral. Ironically, it took place at the same time that the club had booked a place at Wembley for the first time since 1953, but it wasn't remotely as important or satisfying. Stan Mortensen, not a Sir or an Order or an MBE, but just Stan, still looks down on the club he loved so much. At least his funeral wasn't renamed 'The Matthews Funeral'. Blackpool's best player alongside the greatest player to have played for the club. What a duo.

Two decades earlier there was another Blackpool player who scored a goal or two. His name was Jimmy Hampson. He was the most prolific goalscorer in the club's history, scoring 252 times in an eleven-season stretch at Bloomfield Road. He was idolised in the town. He had a waxworks effigy of himself on the promenade at Madame Tussaud's, and he couldn't walk down the streets without being mobbed. The team was

Missing at sea – a terrible end awaited Blackpool legend Jimmy Hampson.

WILLS'S CIGARETTES

J. HAMPSON (BLACKPOOL)

virtually built around him and he'd sometimes have as many as three defenders trying to track him. He was fouled mercilessly and was the target man for the brute of a player who had one job, and that was to stop the other from playing. He was as much the public figurehead of Blackpool Football Club at that time as were Matthews, Mortensen, Armfield and Ormerod all those years later. Now virtually no one remembers him.

When asked who was 'the greatest player ever' to play for Blackpool, nearly all the fans choose Matthews. A few will say Morty, others Charlie Adam or Tony Green or maybe Alan Ball. Some may mention an obscure player who they particularly liked; but no one, absolutely no one, ever mentions Jimmy Hampson.

This is almost certainly because there is no one now left alive who ever saw him play. There are no moving images of the man, so we rely on the words of history and the misty photographs of an athlete running down the wing with a defender trailing, or the glare of a man with his arms folded, unused to the intrusion of a camera. There are few, if any, interviews that have survived – and to prove his reluctance to accept and embrace the fame that was bestowed upon him, he very nearly got off

the train returning from the victorious promotion-winning game at Oldham Athletic so as to avoid the thousands of supporters waiting for their heroes. On hearing that many were chanting his name (inevitably he had scored in the 2-1 victory) he wanted to get off at Kirkham but was gently persuaded to stay. His lack of 'personality', in an age when it wasn't expected of a footballer, has not helped the historians keep his profile alive, yet he was another of those Blackpool players who appeared at an opportune time, ready to take on the mantle of the 'Greatest', even reluctantly.

He barely played for England, but that was more to do with the constant presence of 'Dixie' Deans, who was scoring a record number of goals just down the coastline for Everton, and the fact that Hampson also played a proportion of his career in the Second Division. Having said that, the chasm between the top two divisions was not then quite what it is today. Still, he played three times and scored five goals, so he proved his point.

He was bought by Blackpool in a cinema! He was watching a film (the name of which is sadly erased from history) when the entertainment was interrupted by a club official who informed him that they had just paid £1,000 to his club, Nelson, for his services. Blackpool converted him from a centre-half into a centre-forward, and the rest is history, even if it is becoming fainter by the year. Centre-half Billy Tremelling was his on-pitch partner, whose through-balls for Hampson to gratefully collect and despatch into the net were something of a legend even then. He actually scored around 60 per cent of all Blackpool's goals in the period between 1927 and 1938, and then he was gone.

Two days after playing in an FA Cup tie against Birmingham City, he went fishing off the Fleetwood coast. The yacht, *Defender*, collided with a trawler and he fell overboard. He was never found and, at the age of 31, one of the most amazing players to have worn a Blackpool shirt, and certainly rarely matched since, was no longer with us. Grown men cried and prayers were said. Blackpool had lost a player who was everything to the club.

Hampson was a player that was constantly under criticism from the local press, suggesting he had lost his touch, was slowing down or was no longer good enough. He didn't answer except to play in the next match and score, to prove them wrong. The supporters adored him, but the local reporters appear to have had a hit-and-miss relationship with him. Even though he was a legend at the club at the time, his death only seemed to underline his importance to Blackpool, and the team suffered immeasurably afterwards. How do you replace a player who scored between 20 and 40 goals each season? As it was, the Second World War followed and, by the time football returned to normal, it is possible he may have been too old to recreate his past exploits.

During his years he never courted publicity, and time and again much bigger clubs tried to lure him away, Arsenal being the most persistent. It is said that he would not have taken to the 'bright lights' of London (where have we read that before?), but sometimes it is a pleasure to imagine what would have happened, and to what heights he might have climbed in his incredible career. Whereas both Matthews and Mortensen have stands named in their honour at Bloomfield Road, there is no such accolade afforded to Hampson. As it is, Blackpool Football Club has the knowledge that he played for them, and as it is nearly a century since his exploits, it is also hoped that he will never, ever be forgotten. The following report from a local newspaper perfectly sums up the grief unleashed by his untimely death:

'Mrs Jimmy Hampson, ill in a Blackpool nursing home, listened on a bedside telephone yesterday to the memorial service at St John's Church, Blackpool, to her husband, Jimmy Hampson, and Mr Harry V. Newsome, who were drowned in a yachting accident off Fleetwood. By her side sat Mrs Newsome. It was the first time the bereaved women had met. And while the two shared their grief silently together crowds inside and outside the church paid their tribute to the two men. The church was crowded and over 1,000, who could not be found accommodation, heard the service relayed to them outside by loudspeakers. The congregation included the Mayor and Mayoress of Blackpool (Alderman and Mrs J. R. Quayle), members of the Corporation, directors and players of the Blackpool Football Club, members of the local junior football leagues, angling societies, Freemasons, and other organisations.' Monday 17th January 1938

Of course, unlike Hampson, Jimmy Armfield has a stand named after him. How could it not be? The original 'one-club' player, and that club was Blackpool. This was a man who devoted the entirety of his career to his hometown club, no matter how far they were falling from the heights they had previously attained. It is a sad fact that he stayed, and wasn't rewarded as well as so many other players of lesser standing.

Those who remember him wearing the tangerine shirt will recall the lightning pace as he overlapped on the right wing, something he managed to develop after Stanley Matthews suggested it in a practice session. It worked and it became Jimmy's trademark. He played over 600 times for us, never being tempted or lured by any other club. He was Blackpool through and through, a member of his local church and one of those who valued his community. He loved the town and the town loved him.

JIMMY
ARMFIELD
Right Back
Blackpool & England

As a sportsman, he could have been a rugby player if it had called. Instead, he played football and played it very well. In a practice session at Bloomfield Road, where young players would try to impress the surrounding watchers and maybe a few scouts, he was spotted by the manager Joe Smith and was then ingrained into the Blackpool culture.

'What's your name?'

'Why do you want to know?'

'You're doing all right. Would you like to play for us?'

His debut calling was equally as abrupt. He was asleep in bed on the Boxing Day morning of 1954 when Smith called on the telephone.

'Pack your bags. Eddie Shimwell is injured, so you're playing at Portsmouth tomorrow. Goodbye.'

By the following season he had made the right-back position his own, and after the 1962 World Cup was voted the 'Best Right-back in the World'. He captained Blackpool and he captained his country, at a time when neither were enjoying the success he deserved. The only thing he won at Blackpool was promotion to Division One on the night they beat rivals Preston 3-0 at Deepdale in 1970. He was chaired off by the cheering supporters, but it was scant reward for the devotion he had showed. One year later he retired from the game with Blackpool falling back through the relegation trapdoor. As he walked on to the pitch he was given a guard of honour both by his own players and those of Manchester United. In reality, if he lived in the current commercial age, he would have been walking on to that same pitch wearing a red shirt, not tangerine. Within a month, Blackpool won their first trophy since 1953 by beating Bologna

2-1 in the Anglo-Italian Cup final. Jimmy was not there.

At international level Armfield made his debut against Brazil in 1959 in front of an intimidating 120,000 of their own supporters, lifted into an even greater frenzy than normal by political activists who had dropped thousands of leaflets from the sky, meaning a lengthy delay to kick-off. He coped well with his nerves and apprehension. At the time, England were under the curious belief that they were on the verge of becoming the best in the world, yet it was seven years before the Jules Rimet Trophy was lifted at a sunlit Wembley. Jimmy wasn't there, though. He had been replaced in Alf Ramsey's affections by George Cohen and had bowed out of international football the season before. One can only imagine his feelings that day. There was a Blackpool player on the pitch in Alan Ball, who had already declared his new loyalty to Everton; but there should have been a second Blackpool player present, one who would never declare anything other than love for his club.

'Some chaps move from club to club, they're just out to make a fast buck. They can't have many real friends. They must have missed a lot along the way, and I feel very sorry for them. They probably make far more money than I'll ever make in football. It all depends where you pitch your ambition. Is it how well or how long you play? Is it all the pleasure you get from playing? Or is it the money?'

He was a towering force on the pitch, fast and agile, strong and sturdy, but off the pitch he was quiet and unassuming. He became a manager with Bolton Wanderers and Leeds United, leading them to promotion and a European Cup final appearance respectively, but in his later years he emerged as one of the most respected pundits on radio as he explained exactly how a move had taken place on the field, calming the firebrand of the commentator sat next to him. As someone who worked closely with him at that time, he made me smile and he made me proud. There was never a moment when he let me worry about the future of the club, usually after another humiliating defeat to Hartlepool or some team equally unqualified to share the same turf as my tangerine heroes. He just nodded and told me he had seen it all before.

Thankfully, before he died, he was able to see Blackpool in the top flight again with the Premier League season of 2010-11, but by then his illness had taken hold and it was becoming difficult. When he died, the town mourned, the game mourned, and a gentleman was lost. He was never knighted, receiving instead what others may perceive as lesser awards; but that was not the way Jimmy saw it. He was grateful for everything the game had given him.

One of my last memories of him was when I called him one morning and asked if he would write me a short introduction to my last book on the club, *The Complete Record*. He said he would, and then asked if I would 'put the cheque in the post'. I hesitated as I hadn't even thought of offering any money, much to my shame – before he laughed out loud. There was no way he would have expected such a thing. I miss him, telling me to slow down when I was driving too fast in Belgium during Euro 2000 or asking if he was still doing a good job as a radio pundit. The answer was yes, yes and always yes. Far more importantly, the game of football and Blackpool Football Club still miss him today. Gentleman Jim.

In the late '60s Blackpool came across a player who had so much skill and ability that it is now almost impossible to put into words the sheer breathlessness of watching him play. He was called Tony Green. This young Scottish dazzler was inevitably dubbed 'the new Alan Ball' when he signed from Albion Rovers, but that didn't even begin to do him justice. Similar in stature and pace to Ball, Green arrived like a tornado and departed like a tempest. Green was one of the fastest and most exciting players ever to wear a Blackpool shirt, and if there is ever an opportunity to sit down and watch the highlights of his one-man destruction of West Ham United in the FA Cup in 1971,

then take a glass and make sure you savour it. Never has a player so totally and completely dominated an opposing team. His headlines from that day were overwritten by the tacky ones surrounding the nightclub antics of a bunch of West Ham players the night before, but the might of Brazil, Hungary at its best and any other top side would have struggled to contain him. It is on the back of this kind of achievement that Tony Green's story turns into probably one of the saddest.

He played throughout the first two years after making his debut against West Bromwich Albion in a relegated side at the end of the 1966-67 season. He was the force that manager Stan Mortensen relied on as the club reached the promotion line, only to see it moved a little further away at Huddersfield in the last match of the season. Then Morty was

sacked, and Green suffered a career-ending injury in a training session. No one touched him, but his tendon had snapped. He was out of football for over a year but returned against League champions Everton in the First Division, and had the game of his life. He played for Scotland at Wembley against England and on his debut stood higher than anyone else in a blue shirt, despite his size. Blackpool were never going to contain him.

The bids came, but the board stood firm. Newcastle United went to Italy to watch him in the Anglo-Italian Cup final and made a bid immediately after the game, but others wanted him too. Green just kept on playing, but it was inevitable. Bloomfield Road wasn't a big enough stage. Blackpool could never match his talent and his ambition, and so he played his final game in tangerine against Aston Villa in a League Cup tie. I vividly remember saying to my dad that Green might play badly so that he didn't have to leave, as most fans thought the club was cashing in. I was young and, as they say, naïve. Green was outstanding. Of course he was. He even scored, and there was no one in the 20,000 crowd who would deny him his dream move.

£90,000 and Keith Dyson was what it took to lure Tony Green to the north-east and the hotbed of football passion that is Newcastle United. He was sad to leave Blackpool, but this was a club that oozed ambition, if actually very rarely doing anything else. His career was set, but it ended within eleven months. After a tackle in a game with Crystal Palace, he suffered a cartilage injury and at the age of 25 his footballing career was over. The Newcastle manager Joe Harvey said it was saddest day of his life when he was told Green was finished.

'I couldn't hope to buy a similar player, not even for twice the amount.'

Tony Green returned to the Blackpool area and became a maths teacher. There is little else that can be added to that sentence. He never seemed to have harboured any hard feelings, but he would have to be an extraordinary human being not to. He was an extraordinary footballer and, for the four years he wore the Blackpool shirt, it twinkled and glittered and flashed by uncomprehending eyes. Tony Green was one of the best.

'There's little Alan Ball on the right wing, running himself daft…'.

The words of Kenneth Wolstenholme during the 1966 World Cup final. Well nearly, but you get the drift. Alan Ball, Blackpool's Alan Ball, was playing at Wembley in the biggest game in the world. He was still a Blackpool player at that time but was effectively an Everton player after a record transfer fee had been agreed between the two clubs. He was the 'first Alan Ball', when his name has since been used to describe a similar player, and there hasn't been another one.

Ball was a midfield terrier, small and temperamental at first, but wise and growing in stature as his career blossomed. He scored goals, too. For two seasons wearing the tangerine shirt he was the club's top scorer. Ron Suart was the manager who gave him his chance, after Alan Ball Sr had gone almost cap in hand to beg for a trial for his son. Ball was at Bolton Wanderers, who had his registration but little else. They said he was too small, so he slunk away on a holiday to his favourite destination and packed his boots as well. After a few days of wrangling between the two clubs, Blackpool figuratively ran into the streets clasping the contract in their fist. They had Ball, and he was the best signing they could possibly have made.

Those who remember him play tend to think of him in the blue of Everton or the red-and-white of Arsenal, two clubs who smashed the British transfer record for his services. They will also remember his performances for England, although he seemed to receive a disproportionate amount of personal criticism after the 1970 World Cup collapse. Some sadly remember him as a manager, not just at Blackpool where he conducted his own public nightmare, but elsewhere too, as it transpired that the Ball magic didn't work unless he was on the pitch himself. When he returned to play for champions Everton at Bloomfield Road in front of a crowd that sat on the touchlines and climbed the floodlights, he was eclipsed by the return of the new Blackpool hero, Tony Green. It didn't matter, though. Alan Ball had given everything and more to the tangerine cause.

A memory from lifelong Blackpool supporter Roy Atkinson: *'In the November 1964 2-1 home defeat to Manchester United, the 31,000 fans watched in amusement as Ball, full of the arrogance of youth and talent, sat on the ball near the old players' tunnel and gestured for Denis Law to get it off him. A minute later, Law was walking down that tunnel to his dressing-room after kicking both the balls (sic) and being sent off'.* Never today. It was for the moment. Never today.

He was, and still is, one of the best players ever to grace Bloomfield Road.

Some younger supporters will almost inevitably argue with that last sentence and almost inevitably state the case for Charlie Adam. It is a good case to state. Adam was a revelation, a hurricane blowing through the stadium, a typhoon that captured everyone around him and dared them to reach his level. Anyone who saw his equalising free-kick against Cardiff City in the Wembley Play-off final would just drop their jaw and stand open-mouthed. Anyone who wasn't a Blackpool supporter, that is. We all knew what he could do, and for a while he was our little secret.

Adam arrived before Holloway, yet the two have become intrinsically linked in Blackpool folklore. On loan from Rangers, he produced performances, especially at Deepdale against Preston, that cemented a legendary status. It was the Latvian investor Valeri Belokon who recognised his worth and put up the money for his permanent transfer to the seaside. If ever money was well spent.

Sir Alex Ferguson, a pretty good judge of football, said after his team had somehow been presented with a comeback victory over Blackpool in the Premier League season courtesy of a referee who presumably didn't

understand the handball law, or couldn't quite accept that Blackpool might go 3-0 up, 'His corners alone are worth £20 million…'

They were, plus his eighth-of-an-inch perfect crossfield balls, his curling shots that rippled the netting, his presence, his everything… Charlie Adam was Blackpool FC in that crazy, wacky and please-don't-let-me-ever-forget season. He strutted across the pitch, dominating opponents who called the top flight their natural home. He never looked out of place in a team that had to be grabbed by the scruff of the neck by Ian Holloway as they stared awe-bound at the rising grandstands. He looked like he belonged there, and indeed he did. After the floor fell beneath Blackpool in an agonising and tortuous way, Adam finally achieved his dream move, one that was denied him earlier in the season due to the vagaries of an owner, a fax machine and perfectly bad timing. He went to Liverpool, to a ground where he had dominated a few months previously as Blackpool had given the Reds a footballing lesson.

Adam was more than just a player for the club. He was an unofficial spokesman. The tacky dealings with the chairman (aren't they all?) over non-payment of bonuses, at a time when Holloway was trying to put together a squad to play in the world's richest league, showed that he wouldn't be pushed around. Scottish and tough.

Ever since Charlie Adam left the club, there has been a vociferous cry from many fans for his return in some capacity. One day, it may happen. There wouldn't be a more welcome face at Bloomfield Road.

Ray Charnley, like Hampson and Mortensen, was a man who could score a goal or two. 222 for Blackpool, in fact. This makes him the club's third highest scorer behind those two, yet his goals came in a team that struggled virtually every single season he played. With an oval smile that matched the oval white lining on his tangerine shirt, a stiff back and a loping style, Charnley confused the hell out of opponents. He was brought on as a striker by Joe Smith and his all-over-the-pitch style (so similar to Morty) meant that no defender could really mark him, and bullet headers at the far or near post became a 'Razor' trademark. Leeds United defender Jack Charlton said he hated having to play against him, and Charlton was not a man for flinching. The goals were regular. He was top scorer in eight out of nine seasons and took just 156 games to score 100. He even scored against Real Madrid in a friendly, and not many Blackpool players can lay claim to that!

England only called once, but it was too late in his career, Alf Ramsey seemingly giving in to a campaign by adoring Blackpool fans to include him. He shrugged his shoulders and got back to the business of scoring for the tangerine cause.

When it came to the end, it seemed a sad and unnecessary denouement. Stan Mortensen, hoping to shake up the team after an early-season home hammering by Millwall, dropped Charnley and allowed Gerry Ingram to step forward. It resulted in a transfer request and a move to the club that had rejected him earlier in his career, Preston North End. With typical irony, a week later he returned to Bloomfield Road and scored against Blackpool. He died in 2004, a moment recognised by both Blackpool and Preston fans five years later in the first Fylde Coast derby since the date, when a minute's applause rang out. They knew his worth, and so did the national press, *The Independent* writing this tribute:

'There have been Blackpool footballers who have played more games for the club than Ray Charnley; and there have been men who have contributed more league goals to the Bloomfield Road cause than the tall, rangy Lancastrian centre-forward. But on both counts, from faithful fans of the Seasiders whose memories stretch back half a century and beyond, there would have to come the heartfelt and grateful rider: not many.'

Every set of supporters has created a collective image of a player or a manager who has transcended mere human frailty into something

Alan 'The King' Suddick
– practice
makes perfect.

BLACKPOOL

Alan Suddick
INSIDE FORWARD

other-worldly and now completely untouchable. For Liverpool fans, it is probably Bill Shankly and maybe Kenny Dalglish, Manchester United supporters might point to Matt Busby and Bobby Charlton, with Arsenal fans looking at George Graham and Ian Wright. For Blackpool's long-suffering, loyal followers, it is almost definitely Billy Ayre and Alan Suddick. Ayre never made a bad decision, never took charge of a bad performance and never failed. It is the same for Alan Suddick. He never played a bad game, never sent a pass astray and never once played in a tangerine shirt without pride. He was the 'King of the Kop' as Ayre was the 'King of Bloomfield Road'.

Suddick was an enigma, though. Like all brilliantly talented footballers, he could just go 'missing' without the lightest of footprints left on the pitch he had been strolling around for 90 minutes. Then again, he was one of the most stylish and creative players ever seen at the club, and was the architect, the designer and the builder of some of the most awe-inspiring and simply unforgettable moments at Bloomfield Road in the 1970s – at a time when the club tried so very hard to be the fashionable Chelsea of the north but ended up a fashion victim of the '80s.

Long before David Beckham became the star of an Indian blockbuster, Suddick (or 'The King', as we really should call him) had perfected the art of the banana free-kick, or the bender, or whatever else it was called. There is TV footage of one of these goals in the League game with Oxford United in 1974 at a bleak and virtually deserted Bloomfield Road. Commentator Gerald Sinstadt becomes as excitable as ever after the ball curls into the net at an angle almost unimaginable. In the background there is a young boy wearing a curious quarter-patterned jumper, waving his arms around like he was a windmill. That was me, and I had just seen footballing genius.

His greatest goal is missing, however. Nowhere is there any film footage of what was quite possibly one the most remarkable moments in the history of the stadium. There is a faded black-and-white photo, but it gives no clue as to what had just happened and what was about to happen. It was in the Anglo-Italian Cup at home to Verona, where an entertaining 3-3 draw was lifted to stratospheric status by a goal that is almost impossible to describe. Impossible because everyone who was there now has a different memory, and we have all exaggerated it beyond measure. It doesn't need exaggerating, though. It was unbelievable. No one can remember how many times he kept the ball airborne on virtually every part of his body, whilst waltzing past befuddled defenders, before calmly slamming the ball into the net. Was it three times, four, five, six, ten, 20? Is that possible? Well, the next season (on the back of the publicity the goal brought) he walked around the Bloomfield Road pitch *three times* keeping the ball in the air. He stopped because he got bored. Suddick was the King.

He didn't play for England at senior level, mainly because at his peak at Blackpool he was nearly always a Second Division player. He didn't win anything, apart from promotion and that Anglo-Italian Cup, but then few Blackpool players do. He was brought to the seaside after Blackpool recorded their only home win of the 1966-67 season, 6-0 against a bemused Newcastle United, and the club bought their best player afterwards. Peter Suddaby, who played alongside him, rated him as one of the best technical players in the game. Who can argue with a fellow professional who had a fair amount of talent himself?

I met him once. He was my guest at a poorly publicised book signing and, to fill in the boredom, I reminded him of his great games for the club. He was patient and a gentleman. He loved Blackpool and Blackpool loved him. If he had played in today's goldfish-bowl era, he would have been dropped as many times as he would have played. He would almost certainly have played at the highest level, and almost certainly for England as one of the very few creative talents the country has produced. He didn't, and those of us who saw him week in and week out, strolling the pitch in his tangerine shirt before doing something remarkable, will always remember him. When he died, a part of every Blackpool supporter in the era of flares and platform shoes died with him. The King was dead.

Goalkeepers don't normally reach legendary status at a football club, but John 'Budgie' Burridge did. Blackpool were just one of the 30 or so clubs that Burridge played for between 1969 and 1997, but he stayed with the club the longest. He was playing for Workington reserves at the start of 1971 and then, by April, made his debut at Goodison Park against Everton. As a crazed Blackpool fan, I went to the game that had the words 'nothing to play for' written all over it. Blackpool had already been relegated and the previous season's champions had slunk into mid-table mediocrity. The game was goalless, but his display that day, and especially a save from who else but Alan Ball, showed there was a star in the making.

'Budgie' was a showman, an entertainer who boasted of sleeping with a football in his bed. He was unique and eccentric. He performed warm-up rituals that offended many with their radicalness and amused others with their intensity. He drank fruit juice before a game whilst the footballer of the 1970s would have a slice of toast and a cup of tea. He wore gloves that may well have come from the 25th century, such was their distinctiveness, and he cradled the ball as if it were a new-born. Amongst all of this craziness, there was one of the best goalkeepers in England. His  performance in the Anglo-Italian final against Bologna created the kind of press coverage normally associated with the great Italian defenders, such was the impression he made on the local journalists and reporters.

John Burridge played 131 times for Blackpool, far more than for any other club. He returned years later as player-manager of Blyth Spartans in the FA Cup and scared the hell out of the home side before losing 4-3. He was greeted as a returning hero and waved away as the same. Like many of the players in this section, his picture hangs proudly in Bloomfield Road's 'Hall of Fame'. For years he held back the increasingly strong advances of Scottish keeper George Wood, and it is to both of their credits that the transition was as smooth as possible when 'Budgie' moved to Aston Villa. Wood was exceptional, but then he had learnt from the best.

Two decades earlier there was another Blackpool goalkeeper, George Farm, who broke just about every record in his 12 years at the club. Consecutive appearances, FA Cup appearances, first-team appearances, goalkeepers who scored a goal (against Preston, but it was a 6-2 defeat) and anything else at a time when such records weren't pored over or studied or analysed. He was simply Blackpool's goalkeeper, and that was enough. It was enough 461 times, a number only surpassed by Jimmy Armfield. He only won one honour with the club, and of course that was the 1953 FA Cup final, where ironically his performance was under par and criticised. It was not lost on him.

It is said that Farm was the ultimate perfectionist. His own biggest critic. At a time when players would finish their training and head to the nearest pub (where they were probably the manager or owner if they had made enough money), he would stay at Bloomfield Road and get everyone from players to the groundsman to take shots for him to dive and save. If he let in a soft goal during a game, his anger could be seen. His baggy jumper would have its sleeves rolled up above his elbows, his eyes staring into a distant black tunnel, his mutterings audible around the ground. Farm was Scottish and his mentality was total perfection.

He wasn't graceful. Not in the way grace is described today. He caught the ball with one hand above the other, which seems an almost impossible thing to do with success, yet he managed it. Oh, and in those days, goalkeepers didn't wear gloves either. He used his whole body to keep out the ball, and his command of the penalty area was such that only the brave and maybe the foolish would try to win a loose ball as he advanced. Farm was in control. He was hardly ever dropped from the Blackpool team and, incomprehensibly, was hardly ever played at Scottish international level. That was true of so many Blackpool players down the years, missing international recognition and success at their peak. What the world has missed, and what Bloomfield Road has witnessed.

When he left the club in 1960 – and only then after the team had changed their precarious league position from critical to recovering – he joined Queen of the South as a player and then manager with a modicum of success. Far more interestingly, as far as I am concerned, is that he became a lighthouse keeper. There's another statistic. How many players went from keeping goal to keeping a lighthouse? George Farm did. Another Blackpool legend.

The man who succeeded Farm was Tony Waiters, and whereas George Farm had a distinct style, Waiters was athletic and agile. He actually made his debut for the club on Boxing Day in 1959 against Blackburn Rovers (a 1-0 home victory) and effectively replaced Farm from then onwards. He quickly became a favourite at Bloomfield Road, but this was at a time when the goals against column always seemed to be higher than the goals for.

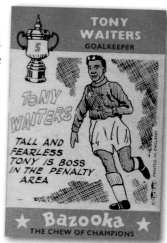

He certainly made an impact though, and by 1964 was making the first of his five England appearances; but like other Blackpool players, his timing for success never came. He'd been included in the original 40-man squad for the 1966 World Cup campaign but failed to avoid Alf Ramsey's player cut and wasn't included in the final 22-man squad. It would have been unlikely he would have displaced Gordon Banks, but the prestige could, and should, have been his.

After that knockback, and with Blackpool's slide into failure, he retired as a player aged just 30 in 1967. He continued in the game as a coach and then as manager of Plymouth Argyle (winning promotion) and the Canadian national team, where they surprised many in the 1984 Olympics.

In the seasons he played for Blackpool they fought relegation annually, and it's fair to say that his talent and command of the area helped the delay before the Second Division welcomed back the Tangerines. He died in late 2020 and was, and still is, remembered by a generation of Blackpool supporters. The club have had some fine goalkeepers in their history, and it's only down to the pressures of space that Burridge, Farm and Waiters are the only greats mentioned. Goalscorers. Let's get back to them, shall we? It is what football is all about, really. Mortensen, Charnley and Hampson, but what about Ormerod or Ellis or Dodds? Just three more names in a pantheon of statistics and records. Most modern-day supporters know of Ormerod and Ellis, but what do they know of Dodds? Jock Dodds? The most prolific goalscorer the club has had. Really? Wasn't that Jimmy Hampson? Well, it was, but Dodds was so prolific that during the Second World War years he scored 230 goals for Blackpool, just shy of Hampson's record and in a far shorter time. Admittedly the opposition may not have been as strong, but just look at these statistics.

He scored eight against Stockport County in the Cup in 1941, and

missed a penalty! Seven against Oldham Athletic and Tranmere Rovers, a hat-trick in under three minutes, another a week later and an absolutely unbelievable 66 goals in 1941-42. This man, burly and heavy, 13 stone of Scottish muscle, was born to play football and born to score goals. Unfortunately, as it was the war, his official Blackpool record is 15 games and 13 goals, which even on its own is pretty impressive. When he left the club after the end of hostilities, he eventually ended up at Everton as a direct replacement for 'Dixie' Deans and helped by scoring 39 goals. He was some player.

Even though he was Scottish and had started his English League career with Sheffield United, he was a Blackpool man. He was quoted as saying that when he came to Bloomfield Road to sign the contract, he walked to the beach '...thought of Sheffield and decided I was in paradise.' After his career ended, he could be seen at Bloomfield Road watching from the seats, undisturbed by the younger supporters who barely glanced his way. Ephraim 'Jock' Dodds was a goalscoring phenomenon.

Players become legends at a club for different reasons. It is usually because of their exploits on the pitch, for their love of the club or the passion they show when wearing the shirt. For Tony Ellis, it was because he left Preston North End and joined Blackpool. Nothing he could do afterwards would spoil that fact, and to be fair there was little he did do wrong. He had actually played at Deepdale in two separate spells, but it was a falling-out with the Preston manager John Beck (a man who referred to Blackpool as 'that lot down the coast' instead of using the name) that forced him to hand in a transfer request. In a moment of sheer joy and unbridled amusement for any Blackpool fan, Ellis played his last game for the Lilywhites at Wembley in a familiar failed Play-off bid against Wycombe Wanderers. The next season, he wore tangerine.

He didn't court popularity. He didn't need to at Blackpool. Fifty-five goals in a three-season period were enough to satisfy anyone, and running on to the Deepdale pitch in a tangerine shirt (despite the inevitable FA Cup loss) was enough for the travelling fans. He was one half of the celebrated double act of Ellis and Andy Preece, with James Quinn lurking in the shadows; but he was also one of the same trio that failed so abysmally in the 1995 Play-off semi-final capitulation against Bradford City. Despite hitting the crossbar in that game, it seemed that the love affair had ended, and soon he was on his way.

My overriding memory of this moustachioed iceman was seeing him score at Brentford in the aforementioned season. It was the winner in a hard-fought 2-1 victory, and as he stood in front of the ecstatic travelling Blackpool fans, he refused to acknowledge them, but instead just pointed to where the ball was in the back of the net before turning away. Class. Simple class.

Brett Ormerod. The only Blackpool player to score in all four divisions. Scored winning goals in two Play-off finals for the club. Missed a whole year with a broken leg yet returned a better player. Joined Southampton for a record fee and played in an FA Cup final, realising Gordon Strachan's ambition to one day sign him after seeing him as an Accrington Stanley player. He joined Preston, but the Blackpool fans forgave him, and his goal in the 3-1 win over Tottenham in the Premier League – giving that incredible record – was celebrated like it was a lifesaving and defining moment. It was. Ian Holloway had started to use him sparingly, but this was his time, and he took it.

Ormerod wasn't a pretty player, but he had pace. He had a goalscorer's ability to see beyond the circle of vision and just sense that there was an opportunity. He scared the opposition despite his slender build, and was able to play at the highest level – for Blackpool fans, and with them. It was justice, you see. When a player like Brett Ormerod does so much for the club when they are struggling, it is perfectly correct that the same player should return and enjoy the glory moments. He had done it at Wembley in May 2010 with a third goal in a breathless first half of football that eventually became the winner. He did it again on a cold night in February against Harry Redknapp's Tottenham Hotspur at Bloomfield Road, and he didn't need to do anything else again.

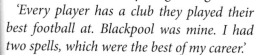

'Every player has a club they played their best football at. Blackpool was mine. I had two spells, which were the best of my career.'

Talking of important goals, there can't have been many more as important as the one scored by Albert Watson in the final game of the 1930-31 season. Blackpool were experiencing their first season in top-flight football, and by the 42nd game were just about on their knees in desperation. From the opening 4-1 destruction by eventual champions Arsenal at Bloomfield Road, to the five separate occasions they conceded another four, or the four times they let in five, or the two occasions they conceded six, or the three games where seven were put past whichever hapless keeper was on duty (nearly always Pearson), or the one stupendously humiliating afternoon where they allowed Huddersfield Town to stroll in *ten* goals, it had become a public nightmare.

The final game of the season saw Blackpool face Manchester City, knowing that relegation was between themselves or Leeds United. The hopeless Manchester United side had been demoted some weeks previously, and so it was a day of hope without knowledge. The transistor radio was waiting to be invented and the only way supporters could discover what was happening elsewhere was by watching the man in the white coat walk languidly to the alphabet scoreboard and put up a couple of numbers for the game everyone was interested in.

Before the game even began, Blackpool had the incredible record of conceding 123 goals in 41 games. That takes some doing, and by the time the 83rd minute came, the half-empty Bloomfield Road was virtually silent – before Jimmy Hampson crossed to defender Albert Watson (surely a reversal of roles that would have been punished by honorary manager

Harry Evans had things gone differently), who simply unleashed and watched in joy as the ball slammed against the netting. Blackpool drew 2-2 and avoided relegation. The strike was then dubbed the '£10,000 goal', as that was how much Blackpool could earn from another season of humiliation in the First Division, which goes to show how times and the economy have changed. It was Watson's greatest moment as a Blackpool player, and even though he scored 21 other goals in his role as a defender, none meant as much.

Blackpool survived another season by only conceding 102 goals, but that was enough. The next campaign saw them well and truly bottom, which wasn't really a surprise. Watson suffered a serious injury and eventually retired in 1935, but by that time he had made 373 appearances for the club. Never a flair player, but stubborn and tough. The goal against Manchester City gave him the freedom of the town, meaning that he was able to dine free at all the restaurants, if he so desired. What a reward.

At the beginning was 'Geordie' Anderson, a Scottish centre-half who joined from his preferred club Blackburn Rovers in 1901. He was described as 'a little worse for wear' by the local newspaper, but that was more to do with his age than any alcoholic consumption. He was essentially a defender, but Blackpool deployed him as an attacker, and he scored the only goal on his debut against Small Heath. Unfortunately, the opposition scored ten times. His role as an attacker was a prudent one as he was the first Blackpool player ever to score a hat-trick, in the 3-3 draw with Barnsley, and then a year later did it again against Burton United. By 1904 his career was over, but he continued with the club and helped many of the younger players, inventing a role for himself that didn't actually exist at that time. He only played 78 times, but this was at a time when there were far fewer matches and injuries were almost always career threatening. His contribution, like so many others, lost in time.

It's obvious that your player won't be in this list. I apologise, but there will always be one that resonates with a fan. For me it was Alan Suddick, one of my two sporting heroes as I was growing up (the other James Hunt), and I was able to spend a pleasant evening with him talking over his greatest goals. He was patient. For Stephen Bowes, it was Paul Stewart:

I grew up on an average street in St Anne's. Nothing Lytham fancy. Three-bedroomed semi-detached with my parents and younger brother Jamie. It was a great place to grow up in. There are loads of things to do in St Anne's as a kid; beach, pier, parks and loads of other kids so plenty of friends with plenty in common. My early love of football was the usual for a young kid. The best teams and best players and I flipped between Liverpool and Man United and singled out Bryan Robson purely because he was England captain. So yes, once upon a time I was a glory fan; not from the area, supported those on TV and newspaper back pages and never went to games. However, this changed sometime in 1985...

My godfather Chris was a die-hard Blackpool fan. He had supported the team since the early 1960s. His father worked as a journalist for the Gazette and got the pre-internet-age rumours. Chris came to the house one day and told us that star striker for BFC, Paul Stewart, was to become our neighbour. Chris lived in a decent house opposite Royal Lytham, yet you would sense a hint of jealousy. My initial reaction was he wasn't Ian Rush; "so what?" I thought. But I was soon to turn to the tangerine side...

Paul had an XR3i. Rusty, noisy, it was a boy racer car. No surprise, though, as Paul was 21, who could blame him. He had a stunning girlfriend, Beverley. Blonde, curly permed hair, size 8... and she had a twin! I was nine, and realised my neighbours were cool and trendy. I convinced myself Paul was going to be my best friend. Who isn't naive at age nine?

I was partially correct. They were cool neighbours but realistically he wouldn't class me as his best friend; that was my fantasy. They were my favourite babysitters. I could beat Paul getting answers watching A Question of Sport, but here's the unique selling point of having a professional footballer neighbour... street soccer.

There were about six kids on our street who were part of the gang. I lost track how many times we would knock on Paul's door: "You playing football, Paul?" He was a pro and couldn't really play because of club rules and insurance. Boring answers to us kids; but these rules were broken, of course they were. We were a very convincing crew. And yeah, we'd play one versus six and get skinned by the pro! If you weren't on Paul's team, invariably you would be rough. If you were on his side, he was your goal celebration partner. They were memories I still remember, great days.

Devastation ensued when he moved to Man City. The Escort was replaced by a Rover Montego. The 'for sale' sign went up and he stayed in St Anne's but went to a four-bedroom detached and, sadly, the street football ended.

When we played City in the FA Cup in 1988, remember the goalmouth scramble? Paul, now my ex neighbour and ex 'best friend', came to the West Stand wall where I stood and kindly gave me a full Man City signed programme. And a week later in the replay, he had helped knock us out the Cup. Thanks mate!'

So, who appears at the end? The story of Blackpool's players will continue for as long as the club exists, but who would you include from the last few seasons? I've included no one. I suppose Tom Ince or Barry Ferguson or Kevin Phillips or maybe Jay Spearing, but none of them have had the same impact as the ones I've mentioned. Yours will be missing. This is not a definitive list but a glimpse, a flash in the sky, a bright light to get a snapshot of who was and who wasn't whilst wearing the shirt down the years. I will leave it to one person to explain what it is to be a Blackpool player. This former player asked to be anonymous, mainly because of the obvious problems that every Blackpool supporter is aware of:

'I loved Blackpool Football Club. I loved the fans and their passion. They are special. I know it's easy for a player to say that when he's at a club, especially if he's playing all right, but the Blackpool lot were amazing. They'd done something that no others had done, and that was to stop going whilst the old owners were there. I remember I saw them at a Premier League game years ago, and they just never stopped singing. That's unusual in England because they don't always get behind the team.

'The club was a mess, everyone knew that, but there was something about the place. You felt like you were in something special, no matter what was going on. I looked at the history of Blackpool when I first joined, and I'm ashamed to say I didn't know much at first, then I started to read about the Matthews and Mortensen days, and it was incredible. How did a small club like Blackpool do so well? I think that's what it was all about. All down the years, the club has tapped into something, and it works. I still love Blackpool Football Club.'

The Successes

I t might not come as much of a surprise to all Blackpool fans that there aren't that many. Successes, that is. Despite being one of the most historic and popular clubs in the country, the connection to success has always been tenuous at best. To date, the club has only ever won one League divisional title, three different cups and quite a few promotions (meaning, of course, a similar number of relegations). Success has been an imposter at Bloomfield Road and never really welcomed.

The one League title was back in 1929-30 when the Second Division championship was won, the honour being claimed on the final day of the season following a goalless draw at Nottingham Forest. Since those heady days, Blackpool FC has not come remotely close to winning the major League title – or indeed any other, apart from finishing second to Leicester City in Division Two in 1936-37 and edging to within eleven points of First Division champions Manchester United to finish second in 1955-56, when two points were awarded for a win. No, Blackpool just does not do success. If it is to come, then it has to be through the normal gut-wrenching and heart-failing routes such as play-offs or any other tortuous path that can be taken. Harry Johnston, the great captain of the 1950s, was once asked why the all-conquering side of his era never actually won anything apart from on that famous day at Wembley:

'I sometimes wonder why we never won the league. We had a great chance one season. We were lying about third at Easter with games in hand, but we blew our chances away. I'm convinced that our side was good enough to win the First Division Championship, and it's one of my chief regrets that we never did.'

The comment on being in a good position at Easter and then falling away could easily have been repeated in 1996 when, at the end of March, Sam Allardyce's men were leading League One by a country mile. Everyone knows what followed, and we will return to this subject later in the book. The League is not something that has occupied Blackpool whilst there were cup competitions to concentrate on.

Blackpool have won three cups (four, if you include the War Cup final against Arsenal). The Anglo-Italian Cup, the Football League Trophy twice (in whatever guise it had at the time) and the FA Cup. It is the last that the club is famous for, of course. Whenever a live television FA Cup draw is broadcast, you can guarantee without any doubt that once Blackpool's number has been shown, the words 'FA Cup giants' or something similar will be spoken – even though a modicum of research into the club's association with the tournament would show just a slim five-year period between 1948 and 1953 when they tried to make it their own. For the rest of the history of the club, the FA Cup has been something that starts in winter and usually ends 90 minutes later.

You could argue that a Play-off final victory brings a trophy, so in that respect Blackpool are just about the most successful in England. To date, they have won five finals at Wembley and Cardiff, and lost two. One reached a level of importance that may never be reached again, whilst another was played out in front of a handful of defiant supporters and barely raised a murmur. The Football League Trophies were played in front of sparse crowds in Cardiff, whilst the Anglo-Italian victory (and the loss the following year) seem to be lost in time, as the tournament died shortly afterwards before being brought back to life briefly over two decades later. So that's it, and with that and despite the paucity of glory, we should now take a closer look at the successes that this wonderful football club has enjoyed.

Where else can we start but the 1953 FA Cup final? That early May day has since effectively defined the club, Stanley Matthews and Stan Mortensen. Is there a single Blackpool fan, young or old, who is not aware of the story of that incredible day at Wembley? Does anyone not know of the amazing comeback from 3-1 down with 20 minutes to go, inspired by a Matthews spell of magic that had gone missing up until that point? Does anyone really not know that 'Morty' scored a hat-trick, the last goal being in the final two minutes before the winner was scored with seconds remaining? Is there anyone who doesn't know it was then called 'The Matthews Final'? Surely not, but the fact is, the game was always about the country's best player and his desire to win something at club level with Blackpool. It couldn't ever be about anyone else.

Blackpool, and Stanley, had appeared in two previous finals and lost them both. In 1948 they had competed in what was regarded at that point as the most entertaining game ever at Wembley when they were beaten 4-2 by a Manchester United side that was beginning to find its power. Three years later they were in another, lacking in entertainment or drama, as they lost 2-0 to a Newcastle United side that only had to beat the completely ineffective and otherwise unused offside trap deployed strangely for the afternoon. In the intervening years, the team had managed to reach the sixth round once, losing to Liverpool, but the rest was unremarkable enough not to be bothered with. Then came the 1952-53 season.

The League campaign had promised much and delivered less, as usually seems to be the case right up until the current day. The first home game of the season saw 38,000 crammed into Bloomfield Road for a 1-1 draw with Preston North End (well before the word 'rivals' was used), followed a few weeks later by the incredible 8-4 victory over Charlton Athletic, as has been previously mentioned. Despite finishing seventh, seven points off the champions, Arsenal (who won the title due to their goal difference being slightly better than Preston's), they never really looked like true challengers. So instead, they concentrated on the Cup!

It all started on a fog-bound, cold and dreary January day at Hillsborough against Sheffield Wednesday. 60,000 fans had packed the ground to watch a Blackpool side without Mortensen, who was recovering from a cartilage injury, giving them a chance to forget the constant relegation battle they were involved in. After 90 minutes and a late winner from Ernie Taylor to make it 2-1, they went back to looking over their shoulder. That obviously wasn't the full story, though. The Blackpool side was lethargic and struggled in the mist, the forward line seemingly off the pace. Wednesday wanted it more. Blackpool didn't let them have it.

Matthews actually scored the opening goal. It was his only one of the season in the Cup and came just a few days after he had been declared fit following injury. A second-half equaliser came from Jackie Sewell, supplied by Derek Dooley – and it was Dooley who gave this interview to the *Daily Mirror* a few days later, when he was asked about 'The Maestro'.

'Matthews played a storming game, harassing our defence and dropping back to help his own. I am convinced that if anyone other than Matthews had been playing on the right wing that day, Blackpool would have been out of the cup... his goal... without pausing to steady himself, Matthews hit the ball into the gap into the roof of the net. I know I would not have scored with such a chance.'

Already, Stanley had made his mark on another attempt to win the medal. Two days later the team learned that they would play Second Division Huddersfield Town at home in the fourth round. It should have been easy. It wasn't. Wet and windy, a packed Bloomfield Road with a large contingent of Yorkshire folk, and Blackpool squeezed through with a late goal, scored more by the wind than the Tommy Garrett shot. Next was Southampton.

'If we can't win it, we don't deserve to stay in it,' was the verdict of the ever-pragmatic Joe Smith. Well, Blackpool didn't deserve to stay in it. They were played off the park by the struggling Second Division side and could only manage to draw 1-1. Beforehand, there was even a doubt the game would happen at all as heavy snow in the Buxton area, where the team often stayed, meant they couldn't get back to Blackpool until Saturday morning after the rail track was cleared, and Southampton's weary players actually travelled through Thursday night and Friday morning to get to the North-West. Such commitment.

'BLACKPOOL IN – BUT THEY SHOULDN'T BE'. The headline on the

back of the *Daily Mirror* the following Thursday said it all. The replay at the Dell, only able to go ahead after hundreds of volunteers had shovelled tons of snow off the pitch, was a one-sided affair. Blackpool had been outclassed and outplayed, yet two goals at the start of the second half from Allan Brown, and an unfortunate own goal, got them through. At this stage, no one who knew anything whatsoever about football would have predicted that this team would be the ultimate winners.

Blackpool in —but they shouldn't be

By BOB FERRIER

IF ever a team should have been out of the Cup that team was Blackpool, who beat Southampton 2—1 in a fifth round replay at The Dell yesterday.
Outspeeded and outclassed by a wonderful first half show from Southampton, two unbelievable goals in the first two minutes of the second half took Blackpool through.

Only in the quarter-final against Arsenal at Highbury did it begin to seem more likely. The story is well known. Blackpool had beaten the Gunners the previous week in the League, but Arsenal were the darlings of the Fleet Street London press. All attention was on them, before and after the game, but it was Blackpool who triumphed 2-1. Matthews was anonymous yet the team were outstanding. Allan Brown's horrendous luck revisited him on the grand stage as he was stretchered off after scoring the winner. It meant he would ultimately miss a trip to Wembley again, just two years after experiencing the first moment of heartbreak in similar fashion. Blackpool played in white shirts and black shorts and Arsenal wore black and white stripes. There was nothing familiar about the game all those years ago. Oh, and a Blackpool fan cycled to and from North London in two days. There will be more of him later. Also, just to prove the point of the media bias towards London, the *Daily Mirror* opined that all would be back to normal come May as Tottenham Hotspur were in the semi-finals, so Wembley would be an easy trip. That was made even more ridiculous by the small matter of Birmingham City standing in Spurs' way. The Blues stood in their way for three games before finally giving in.

There were 20,000 Blackpool fans at Villa Park for the semi-final. There was also the same number of Tottenham followers, but in a ground that in 1953 had a capacity of 70,000, it was of course inadequate. Stan Mortensen returned from injury, but Blackpool were not seen as the favourites. They never were. The game was broadcast on the radio, and the newspaper reports the next day all had a black-edged lining due to the non-appearance of a London club in the final, because Blackpool had won 2-1. They were lucky that day. Very lucky. Tottenham completely dominated the game and should have scored on too many occasions to be accepted by the newspaper reporters. The winner was in the last few seconds of the game when Alf Ramsey incomprehensibly tried a backpass to his keeper, only for Jackie Mudie to collect the ball in the sticky, wet mud and delight the Blackpool fans. It was Wembley time again. The newspapers bemoaned the fact that the final would be anything but glamorous with two dour Lancashire clubs there, but they did concede that Matthews had been given another chance at the age of 38.

'Well, they said I would never get another chance after the 1948 Final. There's always another chance in football.'

Very few of today's Blackpool supporters have probably seen any footage of the 1953 FA Cup final. They will know of it, of course, but the slow-motion, black-and-white grainy film or photographs will mostly be missing from their experience. It is a shame, because that one day in May still defines the football club around the world, no matter what has happened since.

It was a clear day. Wembley was resplendent, the open air and roofless stands basking in the sunshine. The Queen was there on her coronation, live television was present as the BBC had won the argument with the Football Association and paid their £1,000 rights fee, Everest had been officially conquered, the sound barrier had been broken – it was a remarkable time. The FA Cup final just added to the mystique. It wasn't a riot of colour, like today. Post-war austerity meant that clothing was drab and grey, but the tangerine certainly shone. Scarves weren't really known, but rosettes were, or hand-knitted hats. The pitch was green and immaculate, the day was set.

The story of the game has been told over and over. Matthews got his medal. He deserved it for the last 20 minutes, where he suddenly burst into life when it was needed. Mortensen scored a hat-trick. Blackpool recorded the greatest comeback after being 3-1 down and scoring twice in the last two minutes. The game was immortalised for ever more.

If you do watch the full 90 minutes today, it is not easy. The game was slower, fitness levels were not what they are now and watching something where you know the outcome is not much fun anyway. In an age when ten-minute YouTube snippets are just about acceptable, the chances of younger viewers staying with the full coverage are not high; but back in 1953 this was the most dramatic and most exciting sporting event ever.

Nothing had touched it up until that point. Nothing had made people talk as much together in a time when the horrors of war were still fresh in the memory. There was no opportunity to see it again, as video replays just didn't exist. It couldn't be relived, unless newspaper reports were pored over again and again, so for that reason it became more than it was. The final two minutes were made even more glorious and lost amongst all of it was the sheer despair felt by the Bolton Wanderers players and supporters. This is about Blackpool though, so they can share their grief elsewhere. Blackpool had won the most important game in English football, and even today it is still their most famous hour.

The players were heroes. They travelled back by train the next day and got off at Preston to then sit on an open-top bus through the surrounding villages of Kirkham and Poulton, before crawling along the promenade amongst thousands of fans. Matthews, always the gentleman, suggested there had been eleven winners the day before, and not just him. They received their small bonuses and a cigarette case inscribed with their names and the Cup final date, and continued to enjoy legendary status for the rest of their days.

The players who contributed to the only title the club has ever won didn't gain legendary status or receive cigarette cases or even get remembered.

It was only the Second Division championship, after all, even if the gap between the top two leagues wasn't that great back in 1930. At the time, it was a major achievement for the club, but today it is just a sentence in a list of statistics. There was Jimmy Hampson, of course, but there was no manager. Cutting costs meant cutting the manager, so director Harry Evans was in charge, and he didn't do a bad job. Up until this campaign, Blackpool Football Club hardly registered. They had beaten the might of Sheffield United in the FA Cup back in 1906, but that was long forgotten. Blackpool was barely noticed.

The season had been up and down, as had always been the case. Seven goals against Bristol City, six against Preston and Charlton and five against Southampton and Preston (again); but they had lost heavily, too. Ninety-eight goals scored, of which 45 came from Hampson, told its story. The battle for promotion, and ultimately the title, was between Blackpool, Chelsea and Oldham Athletic, and it had resonated with the good citizens of the town. Attendances had started to creep up, with over 24,000 turning up to see the end-of-season battle with Oldham, a game Blackpool won 3-2. Two weeks later, on Easter Monday, they were battling again, this time at Boundary Park. It was cold and windy, as it always is at 'Ice Station Zebra', but it mattered not. Blackpool, inspired by Hampson, won 2-1 and clinched promotion, adding the championship later with a goalless draw with Nottingham Forest. Blackpool were promoted to the First Division for the first time in their history. There was only one man who the supporters wanted. It was Jimmy.

The train shuddered as it left the station, the steam powering the wheels in contained power. Jimmy sat back and closed his eyes, his team-mates laughing and boisterous around him. One of them had pulled out a packet of cigarettes and handed them round, but Jimmy kept his eyes closed. It was supposed to be quiet in a first-class carriage, the heavy oak panelling

breathing serenity and calm for the traveller, but there would be no peace on this journey. Behind them in the second-class, the supporters, full of whiskey and beer, happiness and contentment, were singing bawdy songs, the kind that would make a fair maiden wince. They deserved their moment, though. They had travelled here, and they had enjoyed themselves. This little club. This fine club. They had some good people attached to it. Already he had heard the names of the Arsenal and Tottenham and the Villa, but that was for another day. Now he just wanted to close his eyes.

The train made its way past the soot-covered houses crammed together, the smoke rising from the chimneys. In the next carriage someone blew a trumpet at each passer-by and shouted, 'The Pool are up, you know', much to the bemusement of those watching. They had little knowledge of the game as they hung out their washing and scrubbed their backyard. Football was for those who could afford to take the time to watch, and many had this cold afternoon. Not for them, though. For them it was another train pulling its passengers to another world.

He opened his eyes as the greenery replaced the grey. Fields and trees and hedges with a waving postman on his bicycle. The cows and the sheep walking languidly, taking no notice of the screams of the steam train as it gathered speed. The sky was darkening, the stars twinkling in the blue ink of the night. It was such a change from the afternoon. Jimmy looked and all he could see was the ripple of the netting as the ball, heavy from the dew, scattered the two pigeons sat on the crossbar. He knew then that they would win it. He knew then that they had won it. Now it was done. His tangerine and black shirt, his white shorts and his boots, still caked in the clinging mud of an Oldham day, were all packed away in his bag, ready to be scrubbed and cleaned for next Saturday.

It was the conductor who told him.

'Jimmy Hampson?'

He nodded. He didn't like people addressing him without knowing who they were, but the man seemed kind and smiled as he spoke.

'Train driver says there's hundreds of 'em waiting for you at Blackpool. He was told at the last station. You're a popular fella, my lad.'

'Hundreds? Hundreds of what, sir?'

'Fans, my lad. All Blackpool wants to see you. You're a hero.'

'It wasn't just me, yer know...'

'Tell that to them at the station when you see 'em...'

The conductor walked off. He didn't even ask to see their tickets, but it was a football team. Who cares? Jimmy looked out of the window again.

'Which is the last stop before Blackpool, Billy?' he shouted to his partner on the pitch, Billy Tremelling.

'Kirkham. Why?'

'I'm getting off there...'

There was no stopping him. Jimmy didn't want the limelight. He never had. He waited for the train to pull in to the station, the darkness now hiding the trees that swayed in the breeze. The steam rose from the engine and gathered in clouds under the platform roof before gradually drifting away. He smiled at his team-mates, none of them understanding, but none of them stopping him.

'Are you sure, Jimmy? They all want you.'

'I'm sure. Say something for me...'

And he left the carriage, closing the door behind him, and stood on the platform. It was cold and deserted, and he put his hands deep into his pockets, his Worcester suit only half-heartedly keeping the wind at bay. He watched as the train pulled away and pretended not to notice the supporters who looked at him in horror. They waved and shouted for him to get back on the train, but he just turned away. He had done his bit on the pitch today. There was nothing for him at the end of the line. He just wanted peace, so he walked silently out of the station and climbed into the nearest hackney carriage.

'Can you take me to Blackpool, please?'

'Of course, sir, but it'll be a pretty penny, you know.'

'I know. I just want to get there with no fuss.'

'There was a train a minute ago...'

'...I know.'

'Been anywhere nice?' the driver asked, looking into the rear-view mirror. He thought he recognised him but couldn't place him.
'Not really. I just want to go home now.'
'Right you are, sir...'
Jimmy Hampson. One of the greatest players Blackpool had ever known.

The Anglo-Italian Cup is often mentioned by us Blackpool supporters, but it was an idiosyncratic and rather obscure competition. The fact that Blackpool won it adds yet more oddness and craziness to its history. It was invented the season before the famous final against Bologna, when Swindon Town had been the first victors. It was only really created for the benefit of Swindon, as they had qualified for Europe after winning the League Cup at Wembley. Unfortunately for them, they were Third Division, and teams that low were not allowed to participate in

European competitions, so the English and Italian authorities devised a summer tournament, and Swindon rightly won it (despite the game against Napoli not actually finishing due to crowd trouble). Then came Blackpool.

The competition had some unusual rules, in that offside could only be flagged if the player was in the opposing penalty area, and each goal was worth an extra point. It made for interesting games. It is now no secret that the newish Blackpool manager Bob Stokoe was completely against his team entering the tournament. Blackpool had been relegated from the First Division with Burnley and resembled a punch-drunk boxer who could no longer stand; but Derby County withdrew, leaving Blackpool with no choice as, for some unfathomable reason, they had put themselves on the standby list.

The format was confusing. Six English teams and six Italian teams in three groups, two of each nation in a group, but no team was allowed to play a team from their own country. That meant four games, and the highest points finishers from each country would contest the final. The amount of planning to come to such an idea must have been great, but it was just good to see some summer football at a time when friendly competitions in Hong Kong were not the norm. Blackpool played Verona and Roma at home, and with the exception of the greatest goal ever scored at Bloomfield Road by Alan Suddick in the first game, there was nothing whatsoever to suggest that this cup would offer anything remotely satisfying or memorable. A 3-3 draw and 1-3 defeat seemed to suggest that the return trip to Italy would offer little other than an opportunity for shopping and to taste the local vino.

Italy was different. Whilst Swindon Town were stuttering in their lacklustre defence of a trophy that few cared about, Blackpool were hammering Verona 4-1 (playing only three defenders, so that they could attack and get as many points as possible) and then winning 2-1 at Roma. It was left to the Robins to win 2-1, late on a Friday night against Sampdoria, and so book Blackpool's name in the final. Swindon had failed to qualify by one point, with 14 as opposed to Blackpool's 15.

The final at the Stadio Renato Dall'Ara against hosts Bologna was played in typically steamy conditions in front of a partisan crowd of 26,000. Astonishingly, a few hundred Blackpool fans had managed to get over with little notice, in an era before budget airlines, and they witnessed one of the club's finest hours. A goal down in the first half, only for John Craven to equalise and then a superb Mickey Burns winner in extra-time. That second goal was completely lost on the live television audience in the UK as ITV stopped their broadcast after 90 minutes, totally unable to cope with the possibility that the game might not end at that time. They announced the result at the conclusion of the following programme.

Blackpool had played well and won over the Italian fans, who actually applauded them as they lifted the trophy. Burns had been a star, but so had the reasonably new keeper John Burridge, who had made a string of impressive saves. The result was that for the first time since 1953, 18 years previously, Blackpool had won a trophy.

The next day, in the pouring rain, the players were met by thousands on the promenade and in front of the Town Hall, just weeks after the disastrous relegation season from the First Division. It proved that there was hope and there was optimism, and there was a cup to put in the trophy cabinet.

As an aside, manager Stokoe was not exactly overwhelmed with the Italian players' attitude during the final:

'I have the highest respect for Italian players – as individuals – but they wouldn't do particularly well in English football, because of their temperament and the way they're brought up. The Italians, with all their natural talent, would be great players in English football if they came over here as youngsters and were brought up in our environment.' This was 1971.

The following summer, the club entered as defending champions and reached the final again. This time it was accomplished with some ease, with away victories against Sampdoria (4-1) and Lanerossi Vicenza (2-0), and the return games seeing a 2-0 win against Sampdoria and a whopping 10-0 destruction of poor, hapless Lanerossi. Those of us who were there will remember the goalkeeper leaving the field with 15 minutes to go, and the six goals scored by Mickey Burns. The final against a strong Roma side in the Stadio Olimpico, in front of a larger crowd, was a one-sided affair and Blackpool released their grip on the trophy by losing 3-1.

Twelve months later the club was in it again, and actually won all four games in a completely revised though equally confusing format. They beat Torino and Bologna away by the only goal, and Como and Roma at home 3-0 and 2-1 respectively but lost out to Newcastle United on goal difference. This time there were semi-finals before the final, but by this time most people had lost interest. The tournament didn't appear again until 1992 when it was again radically revised, but still didn't capture the imagination or interest of many. It was a four-year affair in which Blackpool won 11 of the 14 games they participated in and scored 37 goals – which is what the tournament was based around, so naturally they won the cup. A great success. So, what next?

Of course, there is a great story about to be told of that crazy 2010 moment at Wembley. We all know what it was. We will come to the 'Day in Valhalla' shortly, but a similar and just-as-memorable act had to take place first. The second leg of the Championship Play-off semi-final at Nottingham Forest. Evie Morgan remembers it so well:

'I grew up in Nottingham. Despite my local club being a sleeping giant

and my dad's recommendation that I perhaps not follow in his tangerine footsteps, growing up in a house with stories of Suddick's wonder goals and doing my homework on "B.A.S.I.L" (Blackpool Association for Supporters In London) headed paper meant there was only one team I was interested in; so the five-hour round trip became a staple of my childhood.

I can see the City Ground from my bedroom, their bizarre rendition of 'Mull of Kintyre' travels through my windows every other Saturday and, besides the rare County fan, everyone at my school supported Forest. There is something grand about them, they are a huge team in terms of history and impact in the area, and it means their fans have a unique entitlement complex. Not only does this make Forest's recent history all the more tragic, but it has also made my experiences growing up a Blackpool-on-Trenter even sweeter.

Regardless, Blackpool were still seen as a team not to be taken seriously. In the 2009/2010 season, we beat them twice in the league. Famously, after the second game, Billy Davis told the players he'd deliberately lost so they'd get us in the play-offs but this mentality wasn't just Davis', this was the arrogance I would hear daily from everyone I knew. As soon as we got them in the play-offs it was a given, they would win. I sort of bought into it too, kept very quiet that week.

Although we beat them in the first leg, every single Forest fan I knew still thought they'd thrash us at the City Ground. Even though I live a five-minute walk from the Bridgford End, it was impossible to get a ticket. My sister and dad managed to locate singular ones through friends, but being too young to really go on my own we couldn't get me in. Instead, I listened to the game on BBC Radio Nottingham and had friends texting me their taunting messages, given most people I knew were in the home end.

I hear the Forest crowd every single home game, but I've never heard them that loud. The sound of the goals going in beat the radio commentary by a few seconds and Earnshaw's goal was met by the biggest roar imaginable and about a million texts from school friends. I thought at that point Forest fans probably hadn't been all talk and were just being realistic.

In the second half, the only texts I got were from my dad and my sister, most were pretty unintelligible. Like with the Forest goal, I heard DJ's go in before the radio. It's uncommon to be able to hear the away end, but it was unmistakable. By the third goal, it was only Blackpool, clear chants, the *loudest an away end has ever travelled to my home. At one point my sister texted me asking me the score, she couldn't see the board and had lost count. The usually biased and cocky local Notts radio were in awe of us. As with a lot of overconfident fans, Forest have a great talent at turning on their team when the chips are down, but this time it wasn't their loss, it was Blackpool's win. That's how phenomenal we were that night.*

The next day at school I wore my Blackpool coat and scarf, I got a few "well ins" from the County (both Notts and the singular poor Derby fan) but mostly a lot of sighs, disbelief and embarrassment that they'd been so confident. On arrival to my maths lesson my teacher, who had a framed picture of 'Psycho' on his desk, sent me out of the classroom. A bit baffled, I did as I was told, and he followed. He said, "Well deserved, played us off the park, well done," and we went back inside. We humbled Forest fans. I'm not sure many people understand how hard that is, but it's just another reason little old Blackpool are The Mighty.

To this day, my Forest friends talk about that game. DJ and Dobbie haunt them, it's the closest they've been to the Premier League in 20 years. But they all take away the same thing, that we should never have been underestimated, that we were phenomenal and, most importantly, I was right the whole time.'

Winning a Play-off final is also regarded as a success, even though it is matched by the failure of not gaining automatic promotion. Blackpool have done this so many times that some young fans probably believe

it is the only way a team can get promoted. Up to the point of writing, the club has been in seven Play-off finals, winning five and losing two. It is a remarkable statistic and one that isn't bettered anywhere else – and nothing can match or better 2010.

'May 22nd 2010. That day encapsulated 'the dream' of every football die-hard. The occasion, the trip, the atmosphere, the heart-stopping action of the game itself; the elation for us, the utter, tearful despair of the losers – surely no other aspect of

Cheerio, cheerio, cheerio. Only the winners stay behind to cheer at Wembley.

human existence can have so many people in one place feeling such total polar opposite emotions?'

Not my words, but those of lifelong supporter Peter Seddon, and words I totally agree with. In fact, I couldn't have written them better.

How Blackpool got there is still beyond a football pundit's understanding, especially as the team were certain bets for relegation; but the genius of Ian Holloway, the craft of Charlie Adam, the pace of DJ Campbell, the togetherness of a team bought for a silver penny and the passion of the tangerine wave meant that it was a season of being irresistible. From the late-season run of victories (emulating so many before), the second-half performance in the Play-off semi-finals against a Nottingham Forest side that had already been battered three times that season by them, and then wilted under the cascade of a Blackpool hurricane, it was always going to be about the club. The media knew it. The fans knew it. The players knew it. When Cardiff City manager Dave Jones bemoaned loudly in a press conference that 'there are two teams in this final you know', then it was obvious something special was about to happen.

Like the 1953 FA Cup final, the story of the game has been told and relived over and again. Unlike the 1953 moment, this is still fresh in the mind, still good enough not to exaggerate, still the moment when you can say 'I was there...' One person wasn't.

'I was five months pregnant with my second child, and I had bought a tangerine vest to wear because I couldn't fit into my shirt. I had 'baby Seasider on board' printed on it, and I still have it in my BFC collection. Anyway, I'm usually nervous at big games and normally end up watching the game on the TV screens behind the stands as I can't sit still. This time though, I was even worse than normal and as soon as Cardiff scored in the ninth minute, I started having severe pains. I left my seat and went behind the stands. I missed Charlie Adam's free kick! I ran out to the pitch area to celebrate but was overcome with pain, so I was taken by a steward to the St John's Ambulance bay, where I remained for the rest of the first half. They thought I was going into labour! We could hear the cheers and groans through the walls, but no one was giving out any information until at half-time some fella came in and said, 'Your lot are winning 3-2!'. Well, it was a good thing I was lying down. I'd missed all the goals apart from Chopra's opener for Cardiff! The St John's people were happy as they didn't think I was going to have the baby, just that I needed not to get excited and just calm down. Yeah?

I managed to watch most of the second half through my hands and covering my eyes, and was there at full time when the whistle was blown. I could celebrate with the other Pool fans...'

Now can you imagine that? Blackpool's greatest moment in recent times and poor Marie Flintoff missed most of it. Think on this the next time your car breaks down on the way to a Tuesday night fixture at Hartlepool. So, we digress. For Marie and those who didn't see it, the story was simple.

It was hot. It was very hot. There were 37,000 Blackpool fans in the stadium, still the largest travelling number ever to follow the team. The first half was something out of a Keystone Kops cartoon, with defenders racing around chasing a ball that seemed to gather pace each time they got near it. The midfielders were trying to calm things, the attackers felt it was their day in Valhalla. The goalkeepers spent most of the first 45 minutes picking the ball out of the net. Both teams scored three times, but thankfully Cardiff's third was disallowed. The Adam free-kick is probably the most watched YouTube clip in Blackpool, the Cardiff fans taunting before it was taken, only to be silent immediately afterwards. We had all just witnessed genius. Gary Taylor-Fletcher's scrambled goal from a corner and Brett Ormerod's winner made up the first half, and of course it was right that Ormerod should get the goal that would eventually win the game, some nine years after scoring in another Play-off final for Blackpool. This one meant more than a 4-2 victory over Leyton Orient in League Two.

The second half happened. Players were at walking pace, the fans hardly able to stand themselves under a sun that turned the stadium into a glistening ball of orange and yellow. Holloway screaming himself hoarse, Jones looking perplexed, Ben Burgess chasing a ball that was too fast for him as the seconds ticked away. Then it was over. Blackpool were in the Premier League.

It didn't matter that there was suddenly a cash windfall of around £96 million deposited into the account with immediate effect. That was for the suited men looking down. What mattered was that the fans, some who had watched the heartbreak of re-election, crumbling terraces and fellow fans turning their backs, could now say 'Blackpool are Premier League.' Never was a sentence so unlikely.

The celebrations were long and hard. In the new version of the old stadium, the 2010 team linked hands and arms with the ghosts of the 1953 team and added another chapter to the history of the club. The season ahead could be looked forward to, but for now it was all about drinking as much tangerine as possible and not stopping until the Premier League champagne was served on a weekly basis.

Three years previously there were celebrations of equal magnitude at Wembley after Blackpool had demolished Yeovil Town 2-0 in a game that saw their opponents have one shot on goal, and that was near the end of the 90 minutes. It was the day that Valeri Belokon, resplendent in a flash of tangerine, promised Premier League in five years, and we all smiled. It was the end of a remarkable 'perfect ten' victories as Blackpool just ran out of time to snatch the final promotion spot, but they did it in style with an Andy Morrell-inspired 6-3 hammering of Swansea City away from home. Despatching Oldham Athletic in the Play-off semi-finals was easy, and Yeovil proved no barrier whatsoever on a damp and wet Wembley day. When Robbie Williams opened the scoring, all commentators worth their position screamed 'Take That!' When Keigan Parker scored the screamer in the second half, most of Somerset cried. Blackpool were back in the top half of the English footballing pyramid for the first time in 29 years. It almost made you forget the disaster of 1995.

There were others. A bakingly hot Saturday afternoon in May 1992 at a national stadium that was beyond showing its age and was edging towards demolition (even though four days later it hosted the European Cup final between Barcelona and Sampdoria). Billy Ayre needed redemption for the 'worst moment in my life' episode 12 months earlier, and in nerve-shaking and heart-rending fashion he got it with another penalty shoot-out, this time against a Scunthorpe United side who had battled as bravely as Blackpool. It was promotion to Division Two at last. It felt like two promotions as the new Sky Sports-inspired footballing era had begun with the Premier League, and so the other leagues followed suit with a name change. Eventually Division Two would become League One, but Blackpool had said goodbye only to return a year later.

That return came in 2001 at the Millennium Stadium in Cardiff, with a Division Three final against Leyton Orient. The 'rollercoaster' season was never more emphasised than the one with Steve McMahon in charge. There were 18 league defeats and a 7-0 battering at Barnet, where virtually every Blackpool supporter ever born laid claim to attending (I didn't), but somehow we squeezed into the end-of season lottery. Even the final was a microcosm of the season with a Leyton Orient goal scored so early that most fans were still taking their seats. It was a dominant performance though, and the 4-2 scoreline reflected the match. That man Brett Ormerod popped up to score, something he did again to far greater effect nine years later, and McMahon was told by a TV reporter that if he could 'tap into this', pointing to the celebrating Blackpool fans, then there was a great future ahead. He couldn't, and it took longer than expected.

The record-breaking fifth Play-off final victory came in 2017 against Exeter City in League Two, but few of a tangerine persuasion really cared. As the carcass of the club was being picked clean and the matchday wind was blowing across empty seats at Bloomfield Road, the team somehow overcame such problems and reached Wembley again. Gary Bowyer's men were virtually alone though as fewer than 5,000 travelled, many of them given free tickets, and a sense of embarrassment pervaded the ones who sat across from the 15,000 Devon supporters. The boycott was at its peak. The chairman and the owner both believed that success on the pitch would remedy the damage done, but it was never going to. Fans watched in pubs and at home in Blackpool, cheering the 2-1 win, but there was no connection any more. That was a Blackpool team wearing tangerine, but that wasn't Blackpool FC anymore. The ones who had travelled stayed mostly silent, both during the game and afterwards. I watched from another country and couldn't believe that I was missing Blackpool at Wembley, but how could any of us go? Some did, and it is not for this book to judge. They had their reasons, and they will be respected, but there weren't many. It was a final to be forgotten quickly. The players were virtually alone in their celebrations, but it wasn't the fans' fault. The blame was with the owners.

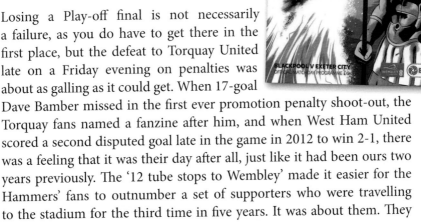

Losing a Play-off final is not necessarily a failure, as you do have to get there in the first place, but the defeat to Torquay United late on a Friday evening on penalties was about as galling as it could get. When 17-goal Dave Bamber missed in the first ever promotion penalty shoot-out, the Torquay fans named a fanzine after him, and when West Ham United scored a second disputed goal late in the game in 2012 to win 2-1, there was a feeling that it was their day after all, just like it had been ours two years previously. The '12 tube stops to Wembley' made it easier for the Hammers' fans to outnumber a set of supporters who were travelling to the stadium for the third time in five years. It was about them. They needed to get back to the Premier League to help pay for the Olympic Stadium they had decided to commandeer. Trevor Brooking was on the pitch, and 'I'm Forever Blowing Bubbles' was played over the loudspeaker. Holloway could have just repeated the words from Dave Jones two years ago. 'There's another team playing today, you know...' Blackpool gave a good account of themselves, and if it hadn't been for nervy finishing and erratic refereeing, then another season in the top flight would have beckoned. Such are the moments of history.

Anyone for the Football League Trophy? Well, in a competition that the club had only once seemingly taken seriously back in 1989 when a Russell Coughlin missed penalty contributed to an aggregate defeat to Bolton Wanderers in the Northern Final, Blackpool suddenly became kings twice in three years. A year after the Play-off success in Cardiff against Leyton Orient, they played a Cambridge United side that was just grateful to have made a final, and who had Lionel Perez in goal. None of that mattered as Blackpool swept them aside and won the Cup convincingly, 4-1. It was of course the first trophy in 31 years for the club and was celebrated by the fans accordingly. It hardly registered anywhere else in the country, but that wasn't important. There was silverware in the cabinet. Just to confirm the new importance of this competition to Blackpool, the club returned to the Millennium Stadium two years later (meaning they matched Arsenal in their three visits in four seasons statistic) and beat a plucky Southend United 2-0 under a roof that kept the torrent of rain off the players and fans. A few years later, the trophy was left far behind, never to be competed for again – until they dropped back down the leagues.

There is one other trophy to mention, and that takes us back to 1943 at the height of the Second World War when football was just a passing distraction to the deprivations and horrors of conflict. That passing distraction attracted over 55,000 to Stamford Bridge to see two of the finest teams in England, Arsenal and Blackpool, compete in the War Cup final.

It wasn't actually a competition at all, but an invitation match between the winners of the northern and southern regional knockout competitions. Blackpool had beaten Sheffield Wednesday whilst Arsenal had overcome

Charlton Athletic, and so the challenge went out. Why Blackpool were forced to travel to London for a game between two regional sides was not really explained, but in a time of rationing and restrictions, it wasn't a matter for the moment. As Blackpool were making their way down to the capital, the Arsenal team were having photographs taken with the trophy – just so they could save time afterwards, it seemed.

Blackpool had one of the best teams in the country, helped by players stationed in the town who were able to turn out for the team as and when they were needed. 'Jock' Dodds was one of them. After the 90 minutes were completed, the *Daily Mail*, obviously not used to hyperbole in any of their editorials, wrote that the Blackpool performance was 'one of the greatest by a football team since the game was invented'. They had a point. The Seasiders were two down within seven minutes and in danger of making one of the most wasted journeys in history, but by half-time goals from Dix and Burbank had made it level. In the second half the tangerine shirts swept all before them and a predictable Dodds thunderbolt, followed by a Bobby Finan tap-in, meant the Cup was going north. It wasn't, though. The trophy wasn't released and was literally never seen again, so that part of the Blackpool trophy cabinet that was reserved for wartime cups is bare. Arsenal actually appeared in three of the finals during the war and didn't win any of them – even more absurd that they should have had a photo taken with it, never mind hoarding it away somewhere. Someone at Blackpool might take it upon themselves one day to ask the Arsenal board if they could at least send a replica so as to save the cleaning of the dust in the empty space.

Success doesn't have to mean winning a trophy. It can come in so many other ways, especially in something as fragile as football. The Premier League season can be described as a success, even though it ultimately ended in failure. Just being there was a success. Just playing on the same pitch as the big teams (and beating them) was a success, and just by taking the relegation battle to the final few minutes of the season surely has to be regarded as a success.

Few Blackpool fans will forget the roar from the away section at Anfield after a now-famous 2-1 victory over a crisis-ridden Liverpool, or the 2-1 return victory to complete the only double of the season. At a time when

Kenny Dalglish was taking the managerial seat for the second time at the club, replacing Roy Hodgson, they were a team in freefall, but they still had Luis Suarez and a group of players talented enough to walk all over the tangerine whippets, snarling and biting at their legs. They couldn't, though. The win over Tottenham Hotspur with the special Brett Ormerod goal, the 4-0 destruction of Wigan Athletic on the opening day, the game transferred because Bloomfield Road wasn't ready, of course. The win at Newcastle United, the refereeing blunders that deprived the team of points against Fulham, Blackburn Rovers, Manchester United on a crazy night, Newcastle United and so many more. The odd decisions by Holloway at Aston Villa where he replaced ten players, yet we still only lost to an injury-time winner; the substitutions at Everton at 3-2 up, only to see the team blown away 5-3 (can someone please tell Everton fans to stop laughing now, please?). All of these things are successes. Even the last heart-rending and ultimately heart-breaking final game at Old Trafford – has any other team had so much stacked against them? A final fixture away at the champions – and the knowledge that Blackpool had been relegated with 39 points, which would have kept them up in virtually every season in the previous ten; or that they'd won as many away games as United, or that they hadn't even touched the relegation zone until the very last moments, or that…. It was all a success. Blackpool shouldn't even have been there, with the finances and the attendances, but they were. Every season, there is one club that doesn't look like it belongs in the Premier League when the fixtures are announced. Blackpool were that

club that season, but they made an act of belonging far more interesting and thrilling than any other club before or after. The nation's 'second team'.

There have been other successes, but all played out on a brief and local level. No one can forget the night of 13th April 1970 when Blackpool produced a footballing fairy tale. Around 20,000 tangerine fans in a crowd of 34,000 at Preston North End's Deepdale. A Fred Pickering hat-trick and promotion back to the First Division after three years of being away. That was the night that the rivalry between the fans began, but after the game the Blackpool players refused to toast their success with champagne. It would have been disrespectful of their neighbours, as the defeat had almost certainly consigned them to Division Three. As William Cartmell, the Blackpool Chairman said at the time:

'It would have been different if it had been any other club than our neighbours Preston. People in this area have a tremendous respect for Preston and still remember the great matches between the clubs when we were both in the First Division.' Different times. Blackpool finished in second place and went up. Preston finished bottom and went down.

CHURCHMAN'S CIGARETTES

R. FINAN (BLACKPOOL)

There was success in May 1985 when over 3,000 Blackpool fans travelled to fellow promotion challengers Darlington and saw a Sam Ellis team that absolutely overwhelmed the north-easterners with goals from Conroy, O'Keefe, Stewart and Deary that saw a 4-0 win and promotion back to the Third Division. The rain, the wind, the travel, none of it mattered. Blackpool had won promotion for the first time since 1970, and the good times were back. It was made even more important when the final points were tallied up and Darlington joined Blackpool with one point less in third place. These are the moments that make a football club and its supporters.

One final achievement, and it is barely recognised, but back in 1937 a 2-1 win at Coventry City gave Blackpool another second-place finish and they returned to Division One, a position they didn't relinquish for three decades – that in itself is a major success for such a small club – helped by 44 goals from Bobby Finan and of course Jimmy Hampson. In a way, that was where Blackpool's success story under Joe Smith actually started.

Success is fleeting, and never more so than when you support a club like Blackpool, so this is a chapter to be savoured.

The Failures

SECOND DIVISION

		P	W	D	L	F	A	Pts
1	Bolton	42	24	10	8	63	33	58
2	Southampton	42	22	13	7	70	39	57
3	Tottenham	42	20	16	6	83	49	56
4	Brighton	42	22	12	8	63	38	56
5	Blackburn	42	16	13	13	56	60	45
6	Sunderland	42	14	16	12	67	59	44
7	Stoke	42	16	10	16	53	49	42
8	Oldham	42	13	16	13	54	58	42
9	Crystal Palace	42	13	15	14	50	47	41
10	Fulham	42	14	13	15	49	49	41
11	Burnley	42	15	10	17	56	64	40
12	Sheff United	42	16	8	18	62	73	40
13	Luton	42	14	10	18	54	52	38
14	Orient	42	10	18	14	43	49	38
15	Notts County	42	11	16	15	54	62	38
16	Millwall	42	12	14	16	49	57	38
17	Charlton	42	13	12	17	55	68	38
18	Bristol Rovers	42	13	12	17	61	77	38
19	Cardiff	42	13	12	17	51	71	38
20	Blackpool	42	12	13	17	59	60	37
21	Mansfield	42	10	11	21	49	69	31
22	Hull	42	8	12	22	34	52	28

S omeone once wrote that 'failure is just a step towards success'. Well, I've no idea who it was, but they were obviously not a Blackpool fan. Despite the club crest, taken from the town, that says the word 'Progress' in bold letters, the failures of the team and the club have far outweighed any fleeting success that has come their way. Where do we start?

If you start at the bottom and make your way up, then that is a good way of dealing with the onslaught of heartbreaking waves that wash over generations of Blackpool fans. If you were one of the tangerine-scarved supporters stood on the crumbling terraces amongst a crowd of just 1,747 in February 1983, then it is fair to say you were watching the club at its very lowest point. Three months later, with only Hartlepool, Crewe and Hereford below them, they had to apply for re-election to the Football League for hopefully the last time in their history. Their low finish had been helped somewhat by being deducted two points for fielding an ineligible player, but the sense of shame and embarrassment surrounding Bloomfield Road was immense.

That game against Colchester United was lost, 2-1 the score, but it was a fixture that attracted so little interest from the Blackpool public that hardly any matchday programmes were printed. They are a rarity today. The attendance is officially the lowest at Bloomfield Road. It was a time when the Blackpool hooligan was a far greater draw than the Blackpool player, and a time when a young Sam Ellis was staring out at the muddy grass, the East Stand virtually deserted and the howling wind muffling the shouts of abuse from the fans. It was at that time that he really must have wondered what he had let himself in for.

For the hardy few who stood shivering on concrete terraces that had held swaying masses of men and their happiness, it was a glimpse into a future without a football club. Blackpool FC was on its knees and very few took the time to give it a backward glance as they walked past. The club did survive though, so in a way that was a success, but how on earth did they get to this position in the first place?

The decline, like a snowball rolling down a mountain, had started in a small way and hadn't been stopped. From the moment the club was relegated down to the third tier in 1978, the white flags of surrender were flown. Players left, to be replaced by others who weren't even half their worth, and the finances sank lower and lower. At one stage a supermarket chain showed an interest in the Bloomfield Road site, with the proviso that the club left and found somewhere else to fail. There were few protests from the remaining supporters and the local newspaper didn't seem to regard it as an important enough cause to rally round. The club was becoming more known for its hooligan followers than for the dizzying skills of Matthews or the lightning pace of Ball. What had gone before was now overwhelmed by what was happening in the present, without the faintest link between the two.

By the time Allan Brown had been replaced by an enthusiastic and ambitious Sam Ellis, the team were ploughing the fields of Fourth Division football, and not reaping any reward. Only 24 players were used during the 1982-83 season, but that was mainly because there were not too many more on the books, and the average number of 2,900 fans watched them lose twice as many games as they won. It is extraordinary that the likes of Hesford, Deary, Bamber and Stewart all played in a team that is officially the worst in the history of the club. It survived though, and within two years had gained promotion back to the Third Division.

Of course, the famous season of 1977-78 is etched on most supporters' minds, at least the ones who lived through it. How a season could have deteriorated so badly and so quickly is a question that no one has been able to answer. At the time Blackpool were relegated, when it made such an impact that it was announced on the mid-evening BBC News by a suitably sombre Moira Stuart, the squad were enjoying a post-season American tour. They had rather bizarrely played Fort Lauderdale Strikers twice and were in Atlanta, Georgia when they heard the news. Thankfully they were out of the country and so didn't have to face the wrath of the fans.

How did this happen? On 14th January, courtesy of a Bob Hatton hat-trick, they hammered Charlton Athletic 5-1 at home. Three weeks later, in the next home game against Blackburn Rovers, Hatton scored four as the team ran out 5-2 winners. They were in the top eight and the promotion push was on. Three months later they were relegated. It was all to do with manager Allan Brown and chairman William Cartmell.

Brown had been a great Blackpool player and had proved himself at managerial level already. He'd even appeared in the James Bond film *On Her Majesty's Secret Service* in 1969. Actually, that's a slight exaggeration. 'Why Brown Had To Go' was the newspaper headline being read by Shaun Campbell, Bond's colleague, who was tracking 007 through the

Swiss Alps. The headline referred to Brown's sacking by Luton Town after he had applied for the Leicester City position. Still, it was a nice addition to an already overloaded CV.

In his first season he had taken Blackpool to sixth place, missing out on promotion by just a point and a few goals, yet in this catastrophic headlong race into footballing disaster, he had struggled to get the Bob Hatton-Mickey Walsh partnership to work as well during the following campaign, and so it seemed that his job was 'on the line' according to a newspaper interview with the impatient chairman. Brown's response was to call him a 'back-stabbing rat' in the local paper, and that was it. Brown was sacked and the team capitulated. One win in the final 15 games, but by the time the season was over, they were still safe. A rearranged game between fellow strugglers Cardiff City and Orient was played out on a Tuesday evening. Anything but an Orient win would keep Blackpool up, and the O's hadn't won away for such a long time... The rest, as they say, is history. A 1-0 victory and the team of Bob Hatton (22 goals), Mickey Walsh (14), Paul Hart, Peter Suddaby and Alan Ainscow fell through the trapdoor that they hadn't had a glimpse of all season. It took 29 years to recover.

This was failure on a scale previously unseen at Bloomfield Road. This was a failure that surpassed anything, and with the sudden rush for the lifeboats during the summer period when nearly every one of the 'big-name' players left the sinking ship that had become Blackpool, the failure continued right up to the re-election season in 1983.

Nothing that happened that season could compare to the events of the 1995-96 campaign. This was a failure that surpassed all others and, even today, supporters who lived through and witnessed the calamitous final few weeks talk of it in hushed and heartbroken tones. At a time when Kevin 'I Would Love It' Keegan's Newcastle United were having a public breakdown in the face of a challenging Manchester United, Blackpool were doing exactly the same thing in front of a lesser foe in Oxford United.

After the season ended, one of the players heavily involved in the campaign, James Quinn, said that it was an awful experience watching as Oxford got nearer and nearer and not being able to do anything about it. Well, most fans would probably disagree. There was something that the team could have done about it, and that was to stop losing important games.

Sam Allardyce was the manager, in his first full-time role, and he had brought a respectability to the team, if not any kind of flair. After a season where mid table had been regarded as success, the team were prepared

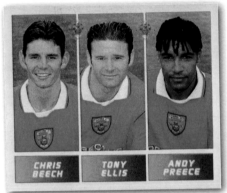

CHRIS BEECH   TONY ELLIS   ANDY PREECE

for a promotion push with the likes of Tony Ellis, Andy Preece and Andy Morrison. It was all going so well. In March they topped the table for the first time since 1978, five points clear of Swindon Town, even though the Robins had three games in hand. Just as importantly, they led Crewe Alexandra by ten, Notts County by eleven and Oxford United were 14 points adrift. At one stage the latter two played out a 1-1 draw in a rearranged game, with County equalising late, and so Blackpool fans were almost certain that promotion was just a grasp away. There was nothing to stop them.

That grasp was limp-wristed though as April, with its showers and its cruel footballing fates, arrived and dampened everyone's ardour. Within the first six days Blackpool had lost twice, 1-0 away at Chesterfield and of course to Oxford United. Two days later on Easter Monday they could have effectively wrapped up promotion by beating Rotherham United at home. They lost that too, 2-1. Allardyce, now looking like a man who had fallen from the sky into a desert and hadn't a clue which way to go, said that Blackpool were in a far better position than their challengers and was happier to be where they were than Oxford and Notts County. Bravado, but the draw at Bristol Rovers the following weekend was celebrated like it was the Champions' League final. All the time, Oxford kept winning.

They drew with champions-elect Swindon Town and still there was hope. They could have been promoted on 27th April at home to Walsall, but by this time the team were frightened rabbits in the headlights of the

Oxford United juggernaut. They lost 2-1 but still there was hope. In fact, at half-time of the final game of the season, away to York City, Blackpool were promoted. They were leading and Oxford were drawing, but like the cat that plays with the mouse, the Oxford players gleefully put four goals past a Peterborough United team that didn't care, and Blackpool finished third by a point. It was almost mathematically impossible to have missed promotion from their position, but somehow Blackpool achieved it.

That should have been it, surely? This capitulation, played out to a local audience as the nation was far more engrossed in the theatre that was the Newcastle and Manchester United drama, was more than any football fan could take. There couldn't be any more. Except there was. Not content with shrouding Bloomfield Road with the fog of disappointment once, they chose to do it again but – as hard as it is to believe – in yet more spectacular fashion. In the Play-offs. The Play-offs that have been so kind to Blackpool FC down the years were the cruellest and most vindictive they have ever been in the month of May 1996.

The first semi-final at Valley Parade was an easy affair. 2-0 winners over a Bradford City side that had finished so far behind Blackpool that they had never been considered promotion contenders. Wembley beckoned. Right the wrongs. Make amends. Everything will turn out fine in the end. This was Blackpool.

After the second leg, the fact that the matchday programme had directions to Wembley printed was used as a suggestion of arrogance, of taking the victory for granted; but in their defence, when else could they print them? In the pre-internet days, there was no other avenue apart from the local newspaper. Whatever the reason though, Bradford manager Chris Kamara, never one to look at a given opportunity and ignore it, used them for motivation. He pinned the offending article on the dressing room door and told his players to read it. It worked.

On the pitch there was a team that knew it was on its way to Wembley glory, and there was a team that shook and trembled, unsure as what to do. Sadly, Blackpool were the latter. I remember my dear old friend David Oates turning to me after the third minute when the referee had waved away claims for a blatant Bradford penalty, and just shook his head. Oatsey and I knew. Most of the Blackpool fans did, too. The 3-0 defeat was probably the most painful 90 minutes of football I have ever experienced. The loss was deserved, though. There were conspiracy theories about how the team had collapsed so easily, but amongst all of them was the fact that Preece and Ellis had hit the bar and Phil Brown was nearly in tears as he collected the ball late on to take a throw-in. Whatever happened is inexplicable. The pubs were busy afterwards, and many fans lost themselves as they dragged their tired minds and bodies back to their loving families, unable to utter a word or nod an appreciation. 'We knew it would come' said Kamara after the game without a hint of self-discipline, 'we could have won by five.'

Bradford, of course, were promoted at the expense of an overwhelmed Notts County team, whilst Blackpool sacked Allardyce on the day that Terry Yorath was given a new contract at Hull City after relegation. It is said that owner Owen Oyston (in prison at this time) had called Jimmy Armfield and asked his advice as to what to do. Jimmy had told him to stick with Sam as the title was there for the taking the next season. Within a few hours Oyston had raised the proverbial axe. I was never able to get the true story from Jimmy in the years I knew him, but it rings true. Blackpool only had another eleven years left of their recovery back to the Championship.

1991 could certainly be described as a failure, and maybe even the following year too, although that ultimately ended in success. The 1990-91 season was pretty dramatic, but aren't they all involving Blackpool? It had started with Graham Carr at the helm, but that didn't last long at all. In fact, just 16 League games. One of those was especially noteworthy. Away at a Halifax Town side that were clinging on to their familiar 'bottom-of-the-Football-League' position, having failed to win at home all season, and the previous Tuesday lost 4-0 at their own ground to the team one place above them, Hereford United. Halifax then put five past Blackpool. Carr's reign was inevitably short. In stepped Billy Ayre, and the rest is of course history for all Blackpool fans as the north-easterner provided a spark that ignited the passion in the club.

That first season under the moustachioed hurricane offered a mixture of delight and despair. Record consecutive home victories and a climb up the League ladder were quite the opposite of anything that had gone on before, though a frailty away from home belied the man who led them. That fragility was never exposed more than in the final game of the season at Walsall. Blackpool had started the game comfortably in the top four automatic promotion places but ended the 90 minutes in fifth. A lifeless and timid performance against a team that had absolutely nothing to play for, in front of a huge, passionate away following, meant a first trip to the recently devised Play-offs.

Once Scunthorpe United had been dispatched, the final at Wembley was against Torquay United, a team who had finished a full seven points behind Blackpool at the end of the season. This was the club's first appearance at the old stadium since 1953, and coincided with the sad loss of Stan Mortensen, so it was expected to be an ultimately satisfying occasion. It turned out to be an absolute nightmare.

DAVE BAMBER
Suffered spot-kick woe in Wembley play-off

Blackpool fans made up the majority of the crowd on an instantly freezing Friday evening in May. Why was it on a Friday? Because the Football League had scheduled it incorrectly, and that was just the first uncharacteristic error on a night that provided little to cheer about. One man, Dave Bamber, who had scored 17 goals in 23 appearances but had missed the late-season run-in due to injury, had a night of football that resulted in the Torquay fans naming a new fanzine after him. He gave away a penalty just before half-time, had a goal disallowed in controversial fashion in extra-time and then missed a decisive penalty in the shoot-out. It couldn't have been any worse.

He wasn't the only one to blame. Blackpool were nervous all evening, despite taking an early lead. Their equaliser was comic-book, with a David Eyres overhead kick crashing off the crossbar and ricocheting off the keeper's legs into the goal, and despite laying siege to the Torquay goal, they never showed the finesse or the confidence to win the game. The penalty kicks after extra-time showed the mental frailty of the players as each Blackpool goal seemed to trickle into the net, whereas Torquay virtually burst the goal. At 4-4, the Bamber miss was inevitable.

As the midnight hour approached, it was the moment that stands frozen in time. A distraught Billy Ayre, never an easy man to interview, uttered the famous words 'I've never had a worse moment in my life, never mind football.' There was nothing else to say.

Although the following season was eventually successful with a second penalty shoot-out Play-off final victory, the failure at the end of the season perfectly matched 12 months previously. Second at three o'clock and fourth at five, after another dispiriting and gutless final-day performance, this time at Lincoln City. What is it about Blackpool and pressure?

Up until 2020, Blackpool had suffered eleven relegations. The League has never really been kind to the club and most campaigns are defined by disappointment. Some of the relegations were heartbreaking, such as from the Premier League in 2011, whereas others were so depressing that the final act felt like a mercy killing, such as 2015. They all sadly deserve to have their individual stories told.

The first time the club was relegated was in 1899 when, after 34 games, they finished third from the bottom of Division Two with 20 points, three adrift of Luton Town. It was only their third season in the Football League, and with attendances a fraction of those neighbours South Shore were attracting, it did seem like the end of the Blackpool story. Despite the best goalscoring exploits of Bob Birkett and Jack Parkinson, they only won eight games all season. One of those was an incredible 6-0 victory over Darwen, but they also conceded the same number four times and lost 7-0 at Gainsborough Trinity. Consistency has always eluded Blackpool Football Club.

Following an amalgamation with South Shore the following summer, Blackpool FC returned to the Football League and stayed in the same division for the next 29 years. By this time, they had made their permanent home at Bloomfield Road (after spending previous seasons between Raikes Hall and the Athletics Ground), had decided on a regular combination of red shirts and white shorts, and had become a limited company. Attendances were still sparse, with a five-figure crowd not achieved until 1908 against Oldham Athletic.

To be completely accurate, it wasn't really their first relegation season, as that term didn't exist at that time. It was re-election, which they failed to gain, so it was the same thing in effect. In any case, they weren't bothered again by the spectre of demotion until 1909, when they finished well and truly bottom, but clearly charmed the footballing committee as they easily gained re-election. Four years later they were at it again. A bottom place finish and another re-election successfully won.

1933 was the second time Blackpool were relegated and, if ever there had been a trapdoor waiting for them, then that was the time. After two seasons in Division One, where they had finished third-bottom twice (conceding 125 and 102 goals respectively), they finally gave up on any pretence of being a top-flight side by finishing bottom of the League with 33 points. Six directors immediately resigned from the club after a vote of no confidence, but the campaign did have its unusual moments. The game with Chelsea at Bloomfield Road was played under one inch of water after 14 consecutive days of rain. Blackpool won 4-0, with Jimmy Hampson helping himself to a hat-trick in a rather underwhelming season total of 18; but in a typical 'hard northerners' versus 'soft southerners' story, only six Chelsea players completed the 90 minutes. The other five either didn't reappear after half-time, or came back on and then walked off again, much to the disgust of the 7,000 hardy Blackpool fans wrapped up in their grey Mackintosh raincoats and dripping flat caps. With terracing that offered little protection due to the lack of a roof, it would have felt like standing under a cold shower for one and a half hours.

FOOTBALL - P. J. DOHERTY, BLACKPOOL

Just to prove that football will always be a 'funny old game', one week after the Chelsea event, Blackpool were beaten 6-2 at Aston Villa, only to reverse the scoreline later in the season. They were still relegated, though. It was after this season that the dark and light blue striped shirts were introduced in the hope of bringing better fortune, such was the innocence of the footballing age. The relegation did at least bring about change at the club, as Harry Evans (who had been standing in as a manager for the last five seasons!) returned to his previous role as chairman, and Alex 'Sandy' MacFarlane was appointed as the new manager on a full-time basis. He dismantled the squad, bought Peter Doherty for £1,000 and transformed the style of play. One door closes…

On Monday 22nd August 1966, around 17,000 mostly Blackpool fans made their familiar journeys to Bloomfield Road for the opening home

game of the season. Some went by bus, some went by car, some by tram and many walked. The English footballing nation was basking in the glow of winning the World Cup just 23 days earlier, and the supporters of the other 91 League clubs were approaching the new campaign with the sense of enthusiasm and excitement that seemed to define the 1960s. The Beatles were about to conquer America properly, the 'flower-power' era of peace and love had been adapted to the young British mentality and the sun had been shining all summer. Seemingly the only ones who couldn't share this rose-tinted vision of the future were the ones who identified with the colour tangerine.

The reason was simple. Just two days after the quote 'They think it's all over...' had quickly been etched into the nation's consciousness, the Blackpool player who had represented England on that dramatic Wembley day was now at Everton. The Goodison Park club, bigger and more ambitious, had bought the ginger-haired genius Alan Ball for £110,000, a new British record, and he was Blackpool no more. It meant the squad, already on the receiving end of an opening-day thrashing at Sheffield Wednesday two days earlier, were now absolute certainties for relegation according to the bookmakers, who were rarely wrong.

Despite the 1-1 draw that night, with the only man who knew how to score a goal in a tangerine shirt in those days, Ray Charnley, scoring, the 'writing was on the wall' – to use an oft-expressed cliché. Blackpool were hardly out of the bottom two all season, and it was no surprise that

Ron Suart resigned in January. He had valiantly tried to fill Joe Smith's shoes for so long, but like trying to hold water in your hand, he saw the legacy of success dripping away year by year. It did bring about the highly popular appointment as manager of one of the club's greatest players in Stan Mortensen, but there was too much work to do in too little time to avoid the inevitable.

It took Blackpool 12 games to record the first of their six League victories, 3-1 away at leaders Tottenham Hotspur – which was amazingly followed 48 hours later by a win by the same scoreline at Chelsea in the League Cup. To prove what a crazy season it was, it wasn't until October that the *only* home win of the season was gained. It was an impressive one, however – 6-0 against a struggling Newcastle United side, where the only decent performer in the black-and-white shirts was a certain Alan Suddick. He signed for Blackpool shortly afterwards in one of the 'buys of the decade' as far as Seaside supporters were concerned.

An even odder statistic was that Blackpool won more games in Merseyside than in their home town, as wins at Everton (1-0) and Liverpool (3-1 in the final game of the season) added to the second victory at Chelsea (2-0) and an incredible 5-1 win at Southampton. (They also beat Manchester United 5-1 at home in the League Cup, to prove how frustratingly inconsistent they were). None of it mattered as they were relegated well before time, finishing a massive 12 points from safety in the era of two points for a win.

Blackpool's relegation from the First Division ended a run of 30 consecutive years in the top flight and was mourned by all footballing purists. The saying that 'The First Division without Blackpool is like strawberries without cream' was repeated often. The club that had graced English football with Matthews, Mortensen, Mudie, Johnston, Armfield and Ball were now trying to keep up appearances in front of crowds of around 15,000 when the nation's football fans were flocking to grounds like never before, hoping for a sprinkling of the glitter dust that had covered England the previous July. Blackpool went down with barely a fight, almost embarrassed to be there, like a boxer who has one too many bouts and knows that his time has come to an end. As the team trudged off the pitch after the final home game (a predictable defeat to West Bromwich Albion), their heads were down, their eyes averted, their legs weary. The fans who made up the crowd of 9,900 (surprisingly, not the season's lowest, reached a few weeks previously with 6,600 against Sheffield United) turned their backs and walked away. This was the lowest moment in the club's history. There were many more to come.

Although the following season wasn't a relegation fight, it certainly felt like one. 'Morty' had transformed the team, selling favourite Ray Charnley to Preston North End and bringing in the likes of Tommy Hutchison and Tony Green. It worked. Always on the promotion fringe, they won their final seven games, including a 'celebratory' 3-1 victory at Huddersfield Town where 3,000 travelling fans invaded the pitch and celebrated promotion. Except it wasn't. In the other decisive game, Aston Villa had scored an inexplicable own-goal in the dying seconds to give Queens Park Rangers a 2-1 win and promotion on goal difference. It could not have been crueller. 0.21 of a goal was the margin, the smallest in history, and of course at a time when the second-chance Play-offs were a long way from being thought of. Blackpool stayed down, and within a year they had dismissed Mortensen. It is also worth noting that if today's goal difference had been used instead of the needlessly complicated measure of goal average, then Blackpool would *still* have stayed down, this time by three goals. It wasn't a failure, but just sheer bad luck. That's Blackpool.

Relegation number four took place three years later, amid the same kind of 'we shouldn't be here' type of mentality. Les Shannon was the manager. He had taken them up in dramatic fashion the season before with the now-famous 3-0 victory at Deepdale, but in the First Division the level of play was higher, the pressure more intense, the chance of failure more likely. In October, with only two victories and eight points gathered, Blackpool played host to Chelsea, the FA Cup holders and title challengers. In that crazy, unpredictable, 'you couldn't write the script' 90 minutes, Shannon, the Blackpool players and fans found a new sense of despair out of the joy and ecstasy of success. Can you imagine what he must have been thinking?

As the manager in his sheepskin coat sits in the far-too-low dugouts on the side of the pitch, he fidgets nervously, he picks at his fingernails, he tries to see the formation of his players through a tangle of legs. He wants to stand and shout, but this is years before the technical area. All he can do is watch and hope that this team, the one that he has trained and motivated and pleaded and pushed with, will at last deliver. They did, but oh it was so brief.

Shannon watches as the team show a level of confidence not seen for a while. Even last week's draw with Huddersfield wasn't at this level. The supporters are behind them, but there's a Chelsea contingent that are there high on the Kop. He shudders thanking that he's not there, waiting for the inevitable. Suddenly Blackpool have scored. It's only on six minutes, but Pickering has just banged the ball high into the net with the keeper off his line. He punches the air and Fred glances at him. It's not a pleasant one. He's still unhappy about the indiscipline charge, but that's for another day. Now lads, keep this going.

The half is a blur. Is this his team? Is this the team that's only one off the bottom? Suddick is commanding, Green is running himself ragged, the defence is strolling. What's wrong with Chelsea? Shot after shot, but we're still at one up. The crowd are singing, but they're not singing his name. It's like they've forgotten that night in Preston, but it was only a few months ago. No matter. Keep on, lads.

Then two in three minutes. Burns has crossed and Fred just smashes it on the volley. The net almost burst, and the crowd almost did, too. This can't be real? It's two against Chelsea. No, he didn't see this coming. Then it's three! It's Suddick, coolly tapping the ball past the poor keeper. He's on his debut, isn't he? Oh, he'll remember this. So will the manager. So will we all. Two goals in the last five minutes and the manager can't wait to get to the dressing room.

He couldn't say much. What was there to say? You can't throw this away, lads. They're finished.

In the second half he twitches, he closes his eyes, his heart beats. There's a sinking feeling, and the stomach churns. There's no real reason. His team *are still playing well but slower and with less flair. That's not what he asked for. He asked them to be careful. Don't let them back into it, because even at three down, they're not suddenly a bad team. Only Chelsea, the kings of comeback, could get something out of this, but don't let them. He watches as Charlie Cooke gets ready and enters the pitch. Does he make his own substitution? No, he doesn't need to. There's only 20 minutes left and it's still 3-0 – except now it isn't. It's 3-1, and they're attacking. They're attacking constantly. He shouts to his midfield to bunch up and not leave spaces. He shouts at Pickering to run after the ball, but there's no response. Make a substitution. Make it or you'll regret it. The team isn't confident. They're being overrun. The crowd is quiet, and the Chelsea fans are making the noise. He glances to the left and sees the mixture of tangerine and blue. It looks like a painting, but he's glad he's not there.*

Fred isn't happy. The crowd aren't, but Pickering is struggling. He can tell. John Craven has fresh legs. It will be fine.

Of course, it wasn't. For those who were there, the last 12 minutes were the worst seen at Bloomfield Road up to that point. 3-1 became 3-2. 3-2 became 3-3 with a minute left. 3-3 became 3-4 with ten seconds remaining, with the most ludicrous own-goal ever seen at a British football ground, Dave Hatton's backpass sailing past Harry Thompson, and Chelsea had won. Later, on *Match of the Day*, John Hollins said that it was the most amazing comeback he had ever played in, and it was down to the substitution of Cooke for Tommy Baldwin that changed the match. Not for Blackpool fans. It was the substitution of Pickering for Craven. They howled their displeasure. Pickering complained publicly and Shannon was relieved of his duties shortly afterwards. Such are the moments of football.

Blackpool were relegated at the end of the season with just four wins and 23 points, eleven adrift of safety. Even a 4-0 drubbing of a West Ham United team (seemingly suffering from a night's activities) in the FA Cup could not disguise the paucity of hope in this dreadful season. At the end of it, Jimmy Armfield retired, given a team salute by both Blackpool and Manchester United players, and the following summer they went and won the Anglo-Italian Cup, but the First Division wasn't a visitor to Bloomfield Road for the next 39 years. Blackpool were not to be missed.

A sixth relegation. It had been coming for two seasons. Alan Ball, one of the greatest players to grace the green (and brown) turf of Bloomfield Road, oversaw a period as manager that was almost completely lacking in any kind of positivity or success. To be fair to him, he didn't actually take Blackpool down to the Fourth Division for the first time in their history, but he was almost completely responsible for it.

In 1979-80, Blackpool, a club almost broken by the too-scared-to-succeed, 'chalk the manager's name on the door' mentality, had appointed Ball as the man to lift them out of the swamp that they were slowly sinking into. Expensive signing Jack Ashurst was struggling, and Stan Ternant had left the club in a blaze of apathy. Ball was the man to change things. Twelve months later he was out, too.

They had struggled throughout the time of his reign, despite the signings of Ted McDougall (who scored for fun on the south coast at Bournemouth, but not on the Fylde coast) and Willie Morgan, neither of whom made an impact. They even designed and wore a new club

crest for a few years with a tangerine tower on a white background (reverting to the old 'Progress' one in 1987), so it was a brave new club that set out on the battleground that was the third tier of English football. Only a late run of good form, culminating in a 2-0 final day victory at Rotherham United, kept them up, but there was no reprieve the next season.

The fans, now disillusioned and far more interested in causing havoc at opposing grounds, turned against Ball. He hardly helped his cause by complaining that most of the 10,000 Bloomfield Road crowd that had turned up for the FA Cup tie with Fleetwood (played there despite being drawn away, as the non-League club's ground wasn't suitable) wanted Blackpool to lose. They won 4-0, by the way. He was sacked a few months later after a defeat to Brentford, and the hapless Allan Brown returned to try and steer the submerging ship into calmer waters. Hapless, because he was left with little to work with, and of course he failed to keep the club up. For the record, Blackpool won nine out of 46 games and only finished above bottom club Hull City by a goal. On 29th August 1981, Blackpool Football Club played their first game in the Fourth Division, a 2-0 home victory over Stockport County, but the crowd of 4,500 was helped by around 1,500 from Greater Manchester.

To prove that if you're going to do something badly, then you may as well do it over and over, Blackpool almost completely replicated their relegation season nine years later, this time under Jimmy Mullen. He had replaced Sam Ellis, once a fans' favourite, but these things are fleeting at Bloomfield Road. Mullen had actually helped the team avoid relegation the previous season alongside Len Ashurst with a late season run-in of form that belied just about everything that had preceded it. He was then given the job on a full-time basis.

There is little to say about the 1989-90 season except that the opening fixture at home to Wigan Athletic didn't see a single Blackpool shot or a corner until the 87th minute. It was a turgid goalless draw, and the road was clear ahead. This was going to be a struggle. The board, mindful of commercial opportunities, had authorised a new shirt design following the successful Dutch side's wearing of a curious zig-zag diamond combination. It looked great on van Basten and Koeman, but on Briggs and Garner it turned to a salmon pink. The only other thing of note was a remarkable FA Cup run that ended in a fifth-round second-replay defeat to Queens Park Rangers, helped by the agreement to host the third game at Loftus Road once more, presumably for financial reasons. Relegation was confirmed with a spectacular 5-0 defeat at Brentford, and the team that saw Andy Garner as the top scorer, with just eight goals, dropped down to the bottom tier for the second time. Mullen left shortly afterwards and then took on legendary status at Burnley, something which baffled the Bloomfield Road faithful. At least the relegation paved the eventual way for Billy Ayre and his remarkable management style.

A decade later it was happening again. After the excitement of the Ayre years, the despair of the Allardyce reign and the jaw-dropping boredom of the Worthington era, Blackpool quietly slipped back into the bottom tier in 2000. Maybe quietly is not the right word, because by this time they had the human bulldozer Steve McMahon as their manager, a man who later famously watched a press conference where the chairman was announcing that the manager had resigned, only to burst into the room and change his mind. The football at Blackpool under McMahon was entertaining, but the antics of the manager were the real ratings winners.

Blackpool were effectively doomed by the time McMahon had replaced the dour Nigel Worthington, who had somehow managed to squeeze the life out of an already untalented team. Despite showing firm resistance to Arsenal in the FA Cup at Highbury, the absolute capitulation at Preston North End four days later meant the walk along the gallows was unavoidable. The damage had been done though, and with Brett Ormerod watching from a distance with a serious leg injury, there was little hope of survival.

That hope was extinguished in the final away game at Oldham Athletic, where an injury-time equaliser brought the travelling Blackpool fans to their knees as relegation was confirmed. Oh, and PNE went up as champions. There are times…

As it was, Blackpool's relegation was probably the best thing that could have happened to them. McMahon looked at it as a huge challenge, and to be fair to him, he rose to it successfully. Winning promotion the following season (albeit in the most tortuous way), two Football League trophies and the desperately slow rebuilding of Bloomfield Road all took place under his watch. None of that could have happened without a drama though, and of course as Blackpool lined up in front of the TV cameras at Kidderminster Harriers on 23rd September, they were wallowing in 91st position, with the commentators asking if this 'famous old club' would go out of the League. A 4-1 win dispelled that possibility, but the 7-0 hammering at Barnet showed that there was a way to go before the team could be regarded as serious promotion candidates. Of course, this is the game that every Blackpool fan who lived at that time attended, so the official attendance of 2,520 has always baffled me.

It might be worth a pause here to reflect on what the club was at this time, at the turn of the millennium. It had been 50 years since their 'glory days' (which actually only amounted to an FA Cup victory, if we were to be extremely harsh) and it was going to be another decade before another glimpse of the pyramid peak. At the time, Blackpool was regarded as a has-been club that played in a derelict ground, with the vultures hovering and ready to peck at the remains. I remember Bryan Hamilton, the former Northern Ireland player and manager, standing at Bloomfield Road, slowly surveying the wreckage of the lack of care and investment, and whispering, 'It's so sad'.

It was sad. The ground was crumbling, although the demolition of the West Stand and the Kop was probably an easier job than expected, and the fan base was firmly stuck in the 5,000 mark. There was little hope that the continuing yo-yo of promotion and relegation between the bottom two divisions was going to change, with the ecstasy of climbing off the bottom rung pretty quickly replaced by the despair of falling back again. That 1999-2000 relegation season had a squad that comprised of Carlisle, Murphy, Ormerod and Aldridge, but also used an incredible 42 players throughout the season. Never has a team been so unprepared for battle, and the change in styles, attitude and belief between the departing Nigel Worthington and the arriving Steve McMahon meant there was little hope of avoiding the drop. Thankfully the latter stayed, and the next few years were fun.

Steve McMahon – just when we all thought he'd gone, he was back again!

'I don't want to stay at Blackpool all my life. Management is definitely second-best to playing, but you can still get a buzz from picking a winning team as with playing. I want to achieve at the highest level.'

He didn't. After Blackpool, he didn't manage in England again.

What else can be said about the Premier League season of 2010-11? Can this be described as a failure, as surely it was a success just being there? It was relegation number nine, and all I know is that walking away from Old Trafford after watching Sir Alex Ferguson play his strongest possible team and bringing on both Owen and Berbatov when the scores were level, were the most heartbreaking and soul-destroying feelings. I couldn't bear to watch United celebrate their 19th title, and I couldn't bear to answer the 'did you stay up?' questions from the red-scarved fans eager to get back down the motorway, despite the on-pitch celebrations and the dressing room tears. There is nothing else to say.

The relegations came quickly after that, but the season of 2014-15 was one that rivalled most in the 'let's have a crisis' stakes. As the club discarded players like confetti, the team predictably weakened to such a state that there was an inevitability about the pending relegation battle; but of course that wasn't even a tenth of the story.

'In the morning it was worse. We only had nine players qualified.'

These were the words of Blackpool's first foreign coach, José Riga, a Belgian who had joined the club from Charlton Athletic, and spent most of his four months in charge wondering why. He was referring to the opening game of the season, away to Nottingham Forest, where it was suggested that frantic contacts between the club secretary and the Football League on the morning of the match were the only reason that Blackpool could fulfil the fixture. As it was, they somehow managed to field a squad of 15, including two 17-year-olds, but lost 2-0. The headline in the *Sunday Mirror* the next day was the simple but effective 'BLACKPOOL SHOWER'. There were reasons for this embarrassment, and they all seemed to involve the Oyston family.

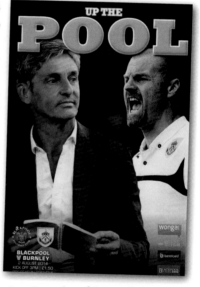

Riga had been appointed to replace Barry Ferguson at the end of the previous campaign, and the club had decided to woo the fans by offering a two-season-ticket offer as part of the 'Riga Revolution'. It seemed a good idea, but they had clearly forgotten to include the manager in their plans, as the summer pre-season saw virtually no activity in the transfer market at all. His backroom staff was non-existent, and after only three weeks there were rumours that he was about to leave. A tour of Spain was cancelled, mainly because there weren't enough players to take, and two friendlies were hastily arranged, but Riga was already at breaking point with chairman Karl Oyston. He had imposed his own media blackout and had stopped talking to anyone apart from his players. The Latvian shareholder Valeri Belokon (who had done so much to help Blackpool's progress since his initial investment in 2006) penned an open letter to Oyston asking for more funds to be made available for players, in which the chairman replied with 'judge me at the end of the season.' Those words were to come to haunt him on more than one occasion.

Blackpool's season was catastrophically bad and matched anything they had produced before. Riga was sacked after 14 games and just one victory (the game highlighted by a walk-out of fans after 53 minutes, just shortly before the winning goal against Cardiff City was scored in front of the TV cameras), but he had seemingly left earlier, only to be found stood outside a closed and empty Bloomfield Road trying to get into his office. In his defence, he never stood a chance throughout his time here, and one  can only imagine the sense of relief he felt when the whole sorry episode was at an end.

Two days later Lee Clarke took over, after having turned down the position a year previously. He immediately dismantled the team of players who hardly anyone had heard of and brought in his own; but that didn't work, either.

'The atmosphere was toxic. There was no way of getting away from it,' were the words of Clarke once he'd left the club. Understatement is clearly a strength of his.

A total of 56 players were used during the campaign – in itself a remarkable achievement bearing in mind there were only eight available two weeks before the season started – and Blackpool won a total of four games and finished 20 points adrift of safety. Their tally of 26 points equalled the lowest points record, but that was down to the fact that the final game of the season, against Huddersfield Town, was deemed a goalless draw by the Football League, despite it not finishing.

The fans, of whom we will hear more later, tired of their protests being ignored and deciding that this was Karl Oyston's 'Judgement Day', ran on to the pitch after 48 minutes after a pre-arranged signal and managed to get the game abandoned. The scenes were ugly; the players ran off the pitch; Clarke shook his head, resigned to the fact that he wouldn't be around for much longer, and the club dropped down to the third tier just four years after leaving the Premier League.

'You could go to a pub team and it would be better run than Blackpool.' Defender Darren O'Day.

'Before the game I noticed Joe Lewis's shirt. It was signed and I thought he was going to do a raffle after the game.' Andrea Orland on the keeper's shirt. It had been borrowed from a fan as there wasn't one available for him.

'Feels like all we achieved will always be a great memory with f@@k all to show for it as a club.' Gary Taylor-Fletcher on Twitter after the relegation.

'We are one of the few clubs in the football world that have no debts and are in profit.' Chairman Karl Oyston.

Just to give some indication of how badly the club had fallen, they went the last 18 games of the season without a victory, having only won eleven of the previous 92. There were heavy defeats. 7-2 at Watford after taking a two-goal lead, and 6-1 at home to eventual champions Bournemouth. Those who were there at Bloomfield Road, as the Cherries tore the Tangerines apart, couldn't help but remember the style of football so reminiscent of the Holloway years. Oh, how times had changed. At Dean Court, in the return fixture, there wasn't a single representative of the club present apart from the coaching staff and players. Whatever respect the club was afforded, was being slowly diminished and erased. There was a feeling that it couldn't get any worse, but it always can.

Blackpool's last relegation (up until the point of writing) was immediately afterwards. Neil McDonald lasted a season and presided over 24 defeats and a return to the bottom division for the first time in 15 years. There was little else to say.

Individual games could be described as failures, and one of the first was on 2nd March 1901. Blackpool were 9-1 down at Small Heath when the referee blew his whistle to end the match, and the downtrodden visitors left the pitch in a state of shock. That was exacerbated when it was found that there were actually still four minutes remaining, as his timepiece was not exactly accurate. The referee took the players back on to the pitch, only for Blackpool to concede another goal, but that was just sheer incompetence as opposed to failure.

Compare that to 27th April 1974 at a Roker Park where approximately 3,000 Blackpool fans ran the gauntlet of Sunderland supporters who knew that a victory would put them back in the First Division. One week previously, Blackpool had overwhelmed Carlisle United 4-0, effectively ending their promotion hopes, so a trip to the north-east was to be a celebration. One up with six minutes to go, and the Sunderland fans, who seemed to take a perverse pleasure in torturing Blackpool supporters by their sheer force of numbers, entered the section behind the goal that was unlocked. Mayhem followed, and very few of the tangerine-scarved fans saw the last six minutes as they were chased out of the ground and through the streets (with the police looking on in amusement). At least they were spared the capitulation and a 2-1 defeat. Carlisle were promoted and Blackpool somehow fell behind Orient and down to fifth.

Are FA Cup final defeats failures? Probably not, but Blackpool lost twice, in 1948 and 1951, before the famous 'history-defining' day at Wembley in 1953. In 1948 they were 20 minutes from winning, before a complete defensive collapse handed United three late goals, but the game was regarded as the best seen on the Wembley turf up to that point. Joe Smith had decided not to choose Jimmy McIntosh, despite him scoring

five goals in the FA Cup that season, and of course a week or so later he was selected for the game with Preston North End and scored five in a 7-0 victory! As an aside, two days after the final, the two teams met in the League at Bloomfield Road, and predictably Blackpool won 1-0.

The opening paragraph of the *Sunday Mirror*'s match report the day after really tells the whole story:

'Manchester United's rousing recovery from near defeat to cup conquest twenty minutes from time, will go down in soccer records as the Manchester miracle – matched only in dramatic incident by Blackpool's collapse.'

Looking at the stuttering black-and-white film of the game, it's clear that towards the end that the blue-shirted Manchester United team were fitter and hungrier for the win, whereas the white-shirted Blackpool side were struggling. Even Stanley Matthews seemed to be tired.

Three years later, in one of the dullest games to have been played as an FA

Cup final, Blackpool lost 2-0 to a Newcastle United team that had Jackie Milburn salivating at the antics of an offside trap that caused a newspaper reporter to call the Blackpool side 'nitwits'. They were comprehensively beaten, with the *'Matthews magic frittered away by Mudie's mediocrity...'* from the same reporter. Matthews was dejected, and maybe the Newcastle win was more to do with the lucky gloves worn by their goalkeeper Jack Fairbrother – given to him by a Preston policeman who supported the Magpies. Thankfully, all the despair was erased two years later.

Staying with the competition, what about the two successive FA Cup ties with non-League Altrincham at Bloomfield Road? In 1984 they allowed themselves to be beaten 1-0 in a dire game, and then just for good measure did it again the following year, this time 2-1. There was the 7-1 humiliation at Birmingham City on New Year's Eve 1994, or the 7-0 hammering at Barnet already referred to. The Premier League season where a 3-2 lead at Everton (whose players and fans, figuratively speaking, fell to their knees in despair as each Blackpool goal was scored, despite the Toffeemen's dominance) only for the most inexplicable substitutions by Ian Holloway and late goals to lose 5-3. The ridiculous 'ten team changes' at Aston Villa the same season, where an extremely poor side beat Blackpool 3-2 in injury time. Holloway was fined by the Premier League and, despite his hero status, most Blackpool fans agreed with it. I even remember a draw against Wrexham at home in 1996. I wasn't there, so my friend rang from the ground at half-time to say that Blackpool were 3-0 ahead. I joked that we would get a draw out of it. We did.

The list seems endless. It will almost certainly be added to.

The Owners

If this book had been written around 30 years ago, then this chapter probably would not have been necessary. After all, who knew anything about the people who owned your football club? They were mostly faceless men who wore heavy suits and drank too much port. They sat in the directors' box and neither cheered nor grimaced, whilst their wives, wrapped up in sheepskin and heavy make-up, sat alongside bored. If your club was in the 'grim' north, these overbearing men normally owned a cotton mill, or managed a coal mine, or lived in a mansion in the Yorkshire Dales. If it was down south, they'd drive a Jaguar, smoke an oversize cigar and have a young lady on their arm. None of this is true of course, but the image of a football club owner was never a particularly positive one, should anyone ever give any thought to it. So, what of the owners of Blackpool Football Club?

It wasn't always the Oyston family. Actually, it was, as they are one of only two owners the club has had, the second being the current incumbent, Simon Sadler. There have been so many people involved with the club at that top level, yet no one person had full control of Blackpool until 31st May 1988 when the businessman Owen Oyston bought the club for a 'nominal fee'.

Like many football clubs that were formed at around the same time, Blackpool had a committee that decided virtually everything, usually over a few pints and maybe some pork scratchings (if they were around in the late 19th century). There is no record of what the original boardroom looked like before the fire in 1917, but a new one was built shortly afterwards before being renovated in 1929 with wood panelling from the old HMS *Foudroyant*. This was a former flagship of Admiral Nelson and was being paraded around seaside resorts in 1897, helping to raise funds for a restoration project. Visitors were charged a penny to be shown around the former warship, but in a heavy storm it was beached, damaging the North Pier. The ship was in such a state of disrepair that it was gradually broken up, with the guns and bells and furniture sold to private buyers. Some 32 years later, the wood from its deck arrived at Bloomfield Road, where it stayed until 2003. Why it took so long to get there is not explained, but it was certainly unique.

If it was possible to somehow return to the year 1887 and sit silently in the corner of the smoke-filled, wood-panelled room where five men of vision discussed the dream of Blackpool Football Club, what would you hear and see? Reverend NS Jeffrey, Sam Bancroft, Dick Swanbrick, Dick Worthington and WJ Brown were the five who were making the first major decisions in the history of the club. We have no real record of what they looked like, although the Reverend would almost certainly have worn a clergyman's outfit, and it is likely that others would have sported the austere and harsh, thick moustache so favoured in those days

– and brought back into Blackpool fashion by Billy Ayre in the 1990s. How they spoke we do not know. What they said we do not know. What decisions they made we do not really know, except to hastily arrange the first competitive matches for the club, choose which players would appear and ask them all if they possessed a jersey that was red so that the team had an identity. It was innocent, and it was the beginning.

Suspend belief (something that is easy when you support this club) and imagine suddenly appearing out of thin air amongst the five. They are sat there in their dark, Worcester suits (except the Reverend, as we have already established), probably smoking a variety of cigars or cigarettes. One may even have a pipe, but the effect is to make the room a hazy grey colour and to give the air a foggy nicotine taste. They are sat around a table, one with a glass of brandy, another a pot of tea, and the Reverend, who favours temperance, a glass of dandelion and burdock. After the initial shock of a human being suddenly appearing in their midst from nowhere, dressed in clothes that are as common as those of an alien from Jupiter, then they listen as you tell them what the future is about to bring. Can you imagine the looks on their faces? Can you see in your mind's eye the shock as you recount every crisis and disaster that is to befall the club that they are lovingly nurturing like a new-born baby? Can you see the doubt in their eyes as they begin to wonder if this is such a good idea, after all?

You see their eyes glisten as you tell the story of the early years, the battle to stay in the newly formed Football League. You listen to the silence as you describe the great players who would wear the variety of colours before the tangerine is chosen.

'Tangerine? What's tangerine?' one asks in confusion.

'It's a colour. It's like orange, but it's not.'

'Oh, I see...' but he doesn't.

You watch their faces light up as you recount the path to glory some 50 years later and the famous Cup final at a stadium they have never heard of, because it hasn't yet been built – and winning the FA Cup in glorious fashion. Then you see their dismay as you describe the fall from grace as the maximum wage is scrapped and the club struggles to keep up.

'Players are paid?' asks the same curious one.

'Yes', you reply, slightly irritated by the interruption.

'How much?'
'Probably it is best if we don't discuss that kind of thing now…'
You recompose yourself and tell the story of the recovery on the pitch, the return to glory, albeit briefly. You shock them when you describe some of the supporters' actions (although the Reverend nods in understanding, muttering about Mr Wilkin from number 23 who has always been a 'bad sort' and had been warned about taking his dog to the playing fields when the game was on), and you describe in detail how the new ground of Bloomfield Road would rise and become one of the most modern in the country before its embarrassing relapse. They know nothing of this. Bloomfield Road doesn't yet exist, but they trust your words.

Finally, you tell them of the men who would follow in their footsteps. The Parkinsons, the Seeds, Hargreaves, Evans, Cartmell and the Oystons. Oh, you tell them about the Oystons…

So, what do we say about the Oyston family that has not been said or thought or experienced? How can we describe a period in the club's history that started with the excitement of a child on Christmas morning, only to end like the mourning bells on a dark and storm-filled night? The only way, surely, is to start at the beginning and try to chronicle the events, both good and bad.

It started well. In the mid 1980s Blackpool Football Club was on its knees, wallowing in the swamp of failure and despair. The ground was crumbling, the team were losing and the locals were ignoring. The famous club was dying, and few seemed to be taking notice. Then, riding on his white charger with a handful of notes held high, came the bizarre-looking figure of a businessman called Owen Oyston. He declared himself a lifelong supporter of the club (although few remembered seeing him there in the past) and he was here to transform it into one of Europe's greats. He bought a small stake and then, seeing the fading faces of the other boardroom members and the lack of desire from the once-loved chairman Billy Cartmell and Ken Chadwick, promptly bought the rest for a very small fee to become Blackpool FC's first official owner. In typical Blackpool style, Oyston didn't attend the board meeting that confirmed his ownership.

Never dressed in traditional fashion, he had made his name, and his fortune, by opening estate agents around the area, investing in radio stations and media outlets, making brief appearances as an actor in a fictional television courtroom drama, and falling into a swimming pool for an advertisement. He was everything that Blackpool as a town was, and everything that the football club needed.

The early years were exciting but promises of new stadiums and entertainment complexes with sliding roofs were just that. Bloomfield Road continued to fall deeper into the ground, its foundations as shaky as the sand on the beach, but a renewed safety certificate and the lowering of the dangerous floodlights kept things going, and another season beckoned. By the time the mid '90s arrived, the chairman still had the support of the fans, despite his public wooing of Manchester United a few years earlier. That failed, wrapped up in the explanation that it wasn't possible to own two clubs at the same time, and he was always Blackpool first, anyway. Then came the imprisonment.

Few Blackpool fans at that stage didn't support him, despite the sentence for rape, and his name was chanted as a taunt to other fans, but it was also a time when on-field activities floundered badly. Money had been given to managers, not least Sam Allardyce initially, but the failure to make League progress effectively tightened the wallet and the budget began to be questioned. Decisions were taken, most of which seemed to backfire, and gradually the tide turned against Oyston and his family.

By this time his wife Vicky had taken control of the club whilst her husband was otherwise engaged, but her popularity never reached above contempt. A fans' protest march to the family home near Lancaster was the start, and after she walked away, tired and jaded, her son Karl took over as chairman – and that is when the problems really started.

It's difficult to know what to say or write about Karl Oyston that isn't negative, yet the first few years were comparatively calm and serene compared to the absolute thunderstorm that was to follow. He took over in 1999 whilst his father was in prison and his mother had shown little desire to continue, but it seemed right from the beginning there was a lack of respect for the supporters, who had been complaining about the way the club was run. In particular, he seemed convinced that his mother had been treated badly, and maybe that was the reason behind the almost complete breakdown in the relationship between club and fans in later years.

In his defence, he can point to the fact that under his chairmanship Blackpool were promoted four times, all in Play-off finals, won the Football League Trophy twice, rebuilt the stadium over a period of time that seemed to stretch far longer than expected, saw Premier League football there, and kept the club in profit. All of that is true, and he was in fact on the board of the Football League as a director. He was a fierce critic of the role of agents in the game, and rarely dealt with them, was respected by other chairmen around the country and seemed to make a penny stretch as far as a pound when transfer dealing. He was almost, *whisper it*, popular with a section of the fans, so how on earth did it go so badly wrong?

His public image left something to be desired. When the delays continued for the building of the South Stand (in a ground that had two sides and a temporary stand) he explained that only '100 or so were missing out' due to the capacity being under 10,000. He said it would be built when he and no one else decided, which ended up not actually being true as it was the eventual intervention of Valeri Belokon that put the project into action (and how the Oystons must have regretted that decision in later years).

As the football on the pitch continued to improve, and Blackpool seemed to be in the habit of winning more than they were losing, the relationship between the chairman and the supporters was almost amiable and friendly. He would often visit the fans' internet messageboards and engage or rile, depending on what mood he was in. I was on the receiving end of a few of those moments, and I've never actually met him! It was all good. The Oyston family were Blackpool and Blackpool were the Oyston family. Then came the Premier League.

There is no doubt in anyone's mind, whether associated with Blackpool or not, that the club was seriously unprepared to sit at the top table. They were not expected to be there and certainly hadn't been invited. They had been relegation favourites, yet had won promotion. They were the club that did not belong. Nevertheless, they found themselves in the Premier League, and during a frantic summer where the list of requirements for Bloomfield Road was not met (the only tick seemed to be that the grass was green, but not everywhere), it was clear they could not start the season at their home ground. They didn't even have underground heating for the pitch, which of course meant postponements that hadn't been experienced before at this level. The early home fixtures were swapped, but it didn't affect the crazy Holloway team that just swept all aside, refusing to acknowledge or respect the norms of new clubs suddenly arriving in the Premier League. Everything was going so well. It didn't last.

Paying bonuses late to players who had successfully avoided relegation the previous season was just bad PR. Having your captain, Charlie Adam, take you to court over his non-payment was bordering on ridiculous, as this was during the Premier League season when in the region of £96 million had been deposited. Not strengthening the team sufficiently in January, when it was clear there was a slippery slope ahead, was the criticism of the fans as they saw the Premier League dream fade – and then a year later seeing an astonishing £11 million payment to Owen Oyston in salary was just about the least fan-friendly gesture imaginable. At the same time, a further £26 million was distributed to Oyston companies, and a piece of land next to the ground was bought at a realistic price, only to be sold back to the 'Travelodge' hotel for an astronomical price. Later in the season, the club's credit card was rejected as the team tried to check into their hotel ahead of a game in the Championship, but oh it got worse...

Social media insults to fans followed, one stating that he was on a 'never-ending nightmare revenge mission' and another where he called a fan a 'massive retard' and 'an intellectual cripple'. He was banned from football for a period of time, and his weekly column in the local newspaper was cancelled with immediate effect. It did not matter. The Oyston family now seemed to be at war with the fans, especially as 'Judgement Day' was now a regular part of the end-of-season celebrations or commiserations. He was pictured smiling stood next to a banner that said 'Cash Cow' in reference to his relationship with the club. He parked a car at the ground that had licence plates that referred to 'Oyston Out' as a way of antagonising the fans, and he had the statue of Stan Mortensen removed before a planned demonstration, despite it not actually belonging to the club. He said it was a meeting place where violence could be planned. It was an act of such utter crassness and lacking in any type of respect for the club's greatest player, that even the most unaffected fan could no longer stand and stare.

His children seemed to revel in the antics of their father, grinning inanely in a photograph with tennis racquets after tennis balls had been thrown on to the pitch during the local derby with Burnley. The relevance of the balls was lost on most, but the effect was successful. Fans were sued. Fans were taken to court. Fans were publicly threatened in an open letter. One, an elderly man called Frank Knight, was fined £20,000 for comments he had posted on social media, but the charity of fellow supporters and the publicity from Russell Brand and Rachel Riley meant he was taken care of.

In a Channel 4 TV investigative news documentary on the state of the club's finances, it was stated by accountant John Frenkel that *'It has the appearance that the club is run purely for the benefit of Mr Oyston'*, and even Ian Holloway (who rarely said a word against his former employers) returned with his new Crystal Palace team and remarked that *'I haven't left much of a legacy, that was my biggest worry, really. If you look at it all, all that is different now from when I arrived, are some sprinklers on the pitch'.* This from the man who helped to bring in the enormous wealth suddenly thrown at the club.

This is a letter sent by lifelong Blackpool fan Stephen Mather to the chairman Karl Oyston in 2015. It has not been edited, but has been 'tidied up' with the permission of the author.

22nd August 2015
To the owners of Blackpool Football Club,
As I sit here looking at my grandad's 1953 cup final ticket, lovingly kept as good as it can in a frame on my wall, I switch my gaze to the tattoo on my arm of my block, row and seat number from another famous game played by the famous Blackpool Football Club, this time at the new Wembley not so long ago in 2010. My mind thinks back to my ten-year-old's first game at

Bloomfield Road, a 6-0 demolition of Ipswich, under the guidance of Olly. After leaving the ground I had to explain to him that we didn't win 6-0 every game! Fast forward three years, we sat together in our usual seats, secured after a promise of a change of attitude towards the football side of a football club. Two-year season tickets to save us some of our hard-earned money; after all, I was always going to attend the home games after being there for the last twenty-three years. My ten-year-old endured the game against Rochdale, which us, a Premier League rich club, were the underdogs. As the final whistle blew, he insisted 'that was it, not coming again Dad'. Broke my heart it did.

So, there we have it, this generation is being lost because of the events of the last few years. A couple of weekends ago I went down to the prom to see the air show here in Blackpool. While there I saw one tangerine Blackpool Football Club shirt, plenty of Manchester United and Liverpool shirts though!

Five years ago, our town and famous promenade were inundated with the unique colour of tangerine, people proud to show it off instead of the usual red. Do you remember that celebration on the prom? All those thousands of people, happy to have been promoted. Wanting tickets, tangerine shirts and goods, willing to buy them because our club was great and successful. The kids of this town, the next generation of fans, the ones we needed to keep interested, loved being part of the tangerine army. We were unique in the football world, nobody came near us, we had such an opportunity.

My friend pointed out to me recently that not long ago, we stood toe to toe with Manchester United, Manchester City, Chelsea and even took six points from Liverpool.

Now look at us. Underdogs at home to Rochdale and then Burton Albion, two defeats later and the generation that includes my 18-year-old and my 10-year-old are no longer interested. It wasn't just these two defeats that brought this on, it's an accumulation of everything that's happened in the last three years. A generation lost to the many red, whites and blues of the standard football world (no disrespect intended).

All I would like to know is, WHY?

Was Olly told three years ago, no more proper investment in the football side of Blackpool Football Club? Is this why he left the club that he helped turn into a unique money-making machine in the football world? Built a team *that took on everyone with confidence and only got relegated through some dodgy refereeing decisions? (shame we didn't play in February and March either!) The team that lost in the last minute to gain promotion once again.*

Was that the moment your mind turned towards an exit strategy, a way to take more money from the club (and the fans) without the football investment?

Is this the plan to get rid of the fan base? Alienate us all, stop people going to the matches? Antagonising as many fans as possible with the stunts and litigation that blight our once proud football club. Is it the plan to reduce the fan numbers so it's no longer viable as a football club? Then you can shut it down, knock it down and build Foxhall Village Phase Three? I'm presuming it's something along these lines as myself and no other Blackpool Football Club fans can understand the happenings surrounding our football club.

This is unprecedented in the history of football all over the world. Never before has a football club been so intensely destroyed from within. Yes, nowadays a football club is a business, owned by private individuals, but you as custodians of these 'businesses' must realise they are more than that. A football club is part of the community, our town changed a lot when Blackpool Football Club was successful.

I presume profits must now be starting to drop. The lack of season ticket sales, downgrading of the size of the stadium, corporate money from home matches down, sales in the shop plummeting, the major cost of policing and fire brigade call-outs at home games, loss of transfer funds received after the last few years' sell-ons.

Please let the fans and the rest of the football world who stand beside us, know what your plan is? If you won't do this then sell the club to someone

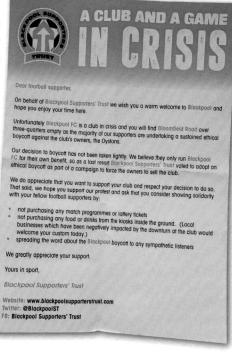

A CLUB AND A GAME **IN CRISIS**

Dear football supporter,

On behalf of Blackpool Supporters' Trust we wish you a warm welcome to Blackpool and hope you enjoy your time here.

Unfortunately Blackpool FC is a club in crisis and you will find Bloomfield Road over three-quarters empty as the majority of our supporters are undertaking a sustained ethical boycott against the club's owners, the Oystons.

Our decision to boycott has not been taken lightly. We believe they only run Blackpool FC for their own benefit, so as a last resort Blackpool Supporters' Trust voted to adopt an ethical boycott as part of a campaign to force the owners to sell the club.

We do appreciate that you want to support your club and respect your decision to do so. That said, we hope you support our protest and ask that you consider showing solidarity with your fellow football supporters by:

* not purchasing any match programmes or lottery tickets
* not purchasing any food or drinks from the kiosks inside the ground. (Local businesses which have been negatively impacted by the downturn at the club would welcome your custom today.)
* spreading the word about the Blackpool boycott to any sympathetic listeners

We greatly appreciate your support.

Yours in sport,

Blackpool Supporters' Trust

Website: www.blackpoolsupporterstrust.com
Twitter: @BlackpoolST
FB: Blackpool Supporters' Trust

who at least wants to save the club, and not allow it to be confined to the annals of history as the first big and famous football club to die!

This year in November is my 25th anniversary of supporting Blackpool Football Club. I wish it would be a happy one but unfortunately it doesn't seem to be panning out that way. I only wish my sons had the same opportunity as myself and thousands of other Blackpool Football Club fans over the years, to have the chance to enjoy the matches and be part of a community asset that brings such happiness to genuine fans who love the beautiful game played in our famous tangerine shirts.

So, to conclude my letter to you, which while writing it feels like a resignation letter. Please let the fans know your plans for our famous club. We've been going to Bloomfield Road for a long time and hope to continue visiting on Saturday afternoons at three. If your plans are to stop this happening, then let us know properly. Stop these circus-like events that blight our club. The rest of the football world should be informed also, and then the FA, the Football League and the Premier league can all see what's happening here, and maybe take their heads out of the sand and address the problem! The other 'small teams' reaching the promised land can see what's happened with the windfall you gain and maybe stop it occurring at their clubs in the future.

If you read my letter from the heart, then thank you for taking the time to do so. If you didn't which I and most Blackpool Football Club fans expect you not to, then it shows the complete lack of communication and respect coming out of our football club towards the customers, the fans, the true custodians of Blackpool Football Club who will always be there.

Yours heartbreakingly,

It had to end. It did. It ended on the 6th November 2017 when a High Court ruled that both Owen and Karl Oyston had operated an 'illegitimate stripping' of the club. They were ordered to pay £31 million to shareholder Valeri Belokon who had brought the court case, and that was it from the Oyston family. Three days later they put the club up for sale after years of saying they never would, and after administrators were brought in, finally Hong Kong businessman and Blackpool fan Simon Sadler bought the club. It was over. Try to tell this story to the five directors sat in the smoky room at the beginning of this 'journey' as it is now commonly called. I will leave Christine Seddon, Chair of Blackpool Supporters' Trust at the time to explain a little more.

'The Oyston ownership of Blackpool FC had always been controversial. From the moment Owen Oyston "saved" BFC when he bought the club for £1 in 1987, there were issues. Supporters complained about the way the club was run and organised protests and campaigns to highlight their concerns. In this, we were no different to the supporters of many clubs who are at odds with their owners. Much of the complaint and opposition lessened when events on the pitch improved and for most of us, expectations were low. The heady days of First Division football were a distant memory, and the reality of lower league football was ingrained on our collective psyche. For years, the Oystons had run the club for their own benefit and whilst most supporters were unhappy at the lack of investment and progress, there was a general acceptance that this was football and there was very little we could do about it.

When Latvian businessman Valeri Belokon turned up at Bloomfield Road in 2006 to sell his beer and ended up with an initial 20% stake in the club, no one could possibly have foreseen the train of events about to be set in motion.

Belokon invested in the team as well as the infrastructure and the improvements were evident from the start. Even the most doubting of Thomas's had to admit that we appeared to have moved into a period of progress. As the team stabilised and then climbed the leagues, culminating in promotion to the Premier League in 2010, crowds swelled, and supporters were happy. This was truly "the best trip" we had ever been on! Alarm bells should have started ringing as early as January 2011 when the old Oyston tactic of failing to strengthen the squad or agree proper contracts with players reared its ugly head. The club had won the football lottery and had unprecedented amounts of money, surely even the Oystons couldn't mess this up?

Relegation from the Premier League followed, but most people agreed we were incredibly unlucky and had performed far better than anyone had felt was possible. In spite of a lack of player investment, the squad that Holloway assembled managed to get us to the play-off final again but this time there was no fairy-tale ending. Supporters were feeling disgruntled and worried at the Oyston attitude towards strengthening and rebuilding the squad. Holloway left in October 2012 and then accounts were published showing many millions of pounds had been removed to Oyston non-football businesses with a staggering £11 million "dividend" made to Owen Oyston. Our worst fears were being realised and the dream of Blackpool FC's future being made secure by that Premier League promotion was fast going up in smoke. It came as no surprise, some years later, to find out that just 24 hours after Blackpool's promotion to the Premier League, Owen Oyston and his inner circle were plotting how to remove vast sums of money from the football club without involving Valeri Belokon or the taxman.

By 2013, with things going from bad to worse, supporters wanted answers and action, but Chairman Karl Oyston refused to deal with anyone apart from the official supporter group, BSA. By this stage, BSA were seen as being too close to the Oystons and so a new group, the Seasiders Independent Supporters Association (SISA) was formed. This new group attracted many members and by 2014 its members had agreed to form an official Supporters' Trust. BST was born and at its first meeting, the venue was so packed with people that two meetings had to be held to accommodate everyone.

Blackpool fans were not new to protest but this was different. The opportunities afforded to the club AND the town through the Premier League monies were being squandered. The club was being allowed to wither and die at the hands of the very people who should have been its

guardians, supporters were ignored and disrespected, and the community abandoned. A meeting between minority shareholder, Valeri Belokon and some members of BST confirmed what we had long suspected. He had effectively been side-lined, the football club monies were being utilised for non-football purposes and there didn't seem to be anything anyone could do about it. The owners' actions may have been immoral, but they were not illegal. Valeri decided to take legal action regarding his 20% stake in the club; we could only hope that this legal action would be a vehicle for change at the club.

The boycott of the club did not happen overnight. As supporters realised that the assets of the club were effectively being stripped, many tried to change things by contacting the club, writing letters, protesting outside the ground, contacting the media – but all to no avail. Some supporters began their boycott of the club and anything Oyston related as early as 2012, when Ian Holloway left, feeling he could do no more without proper support. For others, the decision to act came in 2014 when manager Jose Riga was left with only eight players pre-season and the Oyston attitude towards the club became clear. So many promises had been made over the years, most had been broken, but the influx of the Premier League windfall meant there really could be no more excuses.

By the final game of the 2014/15 season, when an already relegated Blackpool FC played Huddersfield at Bloomfield Rd, a pre-match march and protest attracted over 2000 people. During the second half, some 200 fans occupied the pitch in one of the most peaceful, humorous yet determined protests seen in football and the match was abandoned. Some fans had gone public with their concerns about what was happening at Blackpool FC and the Oystons started their series of legal actions against their own supporters. This was truly the catalyst for the 'Not A Penny More' campaign which followed; the relationship between club owners and fans was already toxic and now was irretrievably broken. There was no way back.

Blackpool Supporters' Trust, the Tangerine Knights and later, The Muckers Supporters Group, led the campaign to oust the Oystons. The injustices done to our club resonated with the supporters of football clubs up and down the UK as well as around the world. The media became interested in this unmatched campaign to boycott the football club and Oyston businesses and before long, Blackpool FC was the talk of the football world. The Oystons became the byword for how NOT to run a football club. Sympathy and support poured in and the boycott grew. By the end of the 2015/16 season, when a two-year season ticket deal had expired, there were fewer than 1500 people regularly attending games. BST manned a space outside the main entrance to the club, calling it their "outdoor office", before every single game in ALL competitions from August 2015 until the end of the boycott in March 2019. At kick off, we packed up and went home. Thousands of visiting fans were leafleted during this time to explain what we were trying to achieve and why it was necessary and maintaining a moral presence outside the stadium felt like the right thing to do. Blackpool fans had not abandoned their club; we were making huge sacrifices to save it.

Enabling the Oystons to continue by handing over our money and endorsing them with our presence inside the ground was not something we felt able to do any more. Owen Oyston refused to budge, in spite of protests and appeals from across the Blackpool community. Our only option was to try and starve him out and to make an example of the Oyston behaviour so that other clubs and businesses would not want to associate with them. Boycotting your own football club is a terrible thing to have to do and Blackpool fans wrestled with their own consciences before making such a difficult and heart-breaking decision. The longer the situation continued, the more determined the boycotters became. Incredibly, Blackpool FC reached the League Two play-offs in 2017 and this was the greatest test of the campaign. The boycott held and the majority of Blackpool fans boycotted Wembley. This was without doubt the biggest visual reminder to the FA, the EFL and the football world of what was going on at Blackpool. This boycott was not a one-off protest or a throwing of toys out of the pram. It was not about League position but was a sustained, ethical campaign, an entire community standing together against great wrongdoing and refusing to be defeated. The temptation of a Wembley final did not shake our resolve.

Meanwhile, Valeri Belokon was moving forward with a legal action against Owen and Karl Oyston and Blackpool FC for Unfair Prejudice. This legal action gave the supporters hope that even though we, as stakeholders in the club, had no recourse to law to resolve the many injustices against our club, as a minority shareholder Valeri Belokon most certainly did. Blackpool supporters attended every hearing between 2016 and 2019 in both Manchester and London. Some of these supporters acted as court reporters *and fed back information to fans at home, covering every minute of these legal proceedings. The supporters attending court behaved impeccably and made a huge impression on the legal teams, the waiting media and ultimately, the Judges. It is unlikely that any civil, financial case has ever attracted so much attention or had so many people packed into the public gallery. The Blackpool supporters and the NAPM campaign formed a large part of the case against the Oystons and huge bundles of documents were dedicated to this.*

Having won the first part of his legal action in Manchester, Mr Belokon moved on to London and the main part of his case. On 6th November 2017, a seismic ruling by Justice Marcus Smith awarded Valeri Belokon £31.27 million. Blackpool supporters were jubilant; surely this would be the end of the Oyston ownership of Blackpool FC? Time ticked by and whilst Owen did make an initial £10 million payment towards clearing this debt, there was then a long period of seeming inaction. Owen claimed he needed time to sell properties and land to raise the money. What became clear was that in spite of pressure from his own family to give up the club, Owen refused to sell up. Although he put the club up for sale, it became obvious that he had no intention of accepting any offers. This was truly the most difficult part of the whole campaign; we appeared to be at a stalemate, and it seemed as if Owen would hang on to the club, even as the rest of his empire crumbled around him.

Blackpool Supporters' Trust, supported by Supporters Direct and the Football Supporters Federation (now amalgamated as the Football Supporters' Association), had been appealing to the EFL and the FA for assistance with the Oyston problem. It was generally accepted that Owen Oyston was NOT a fit and proper person to own a football club due to his rape conviction but the EFL would not apply their Owner and Director's Test (OD&T) retrospectively. Protests outside the EFL headquarters in Preston and London

were arranged and we were joined by fans from other clubs, especially those who had rogue owners of their own. Blackpool fans realised that it was necessary to keep our story in the headlines and to ensure that the situation at Blackpool could not be overlooked. On 6th November 2018, exactly one year since the court ruling in favour of Mr Belokon, BST organised a "Shabby Anniversary" photoshoot. 163 Blackpool supporters came together

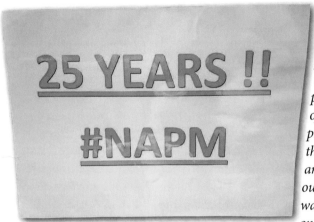

outside the football club on this dark, wet and windy night, one person for each page of the court ruling. Every person held up one page of the judgment for a photograph which was then sent to every national and international media outlet. Blackpool FC was still in the hands of an owner who had been proved to be a rogue but who was still hanging on to our community asset and was killing it in the process. We were determined that this would not go unnoticed.

In February 2019, we were once more back in London for another hearing relating to the non-payment of monies owed to Mr Belokon. Owen Oyston owned land and many properties and the big fear for Blackpool supporters was that he would be able to raise the money to pay off Mr Belokon without selling the football club. The boycott had by now inflicted huge financial damage on the club and it was by no means certain what would happen to it long term if Mr Oyston refused to sell. Step forward Justice Sir Marcus Smith, the Judge overseeing this legal action and the person who had already ruled in Mr Belokon's favour. Justice Smith was a supporter of Arsenal FC, and maybe it was this connection to football that helped him to understand that this was no ordinary financial case. Over the period of this legal action, he had witnessed his courtrooms full of Blackpool FC supporters, clearly committed to their football club. He had been presented with bundles of evidence of the actions taken by thousands of Blackpool fans over a 5-year *period, heard stories of lifelong fans who had not seen their team play for many seasons because staying away was the only collective power we had. He understood that whilst the legal action was between two businessmen wrangling over monies invested and owed, in the middle was a much-loved community asset in danger of being destroyed and a community along with it.*

Justice Smith ruled that Mr Oyston's football assets be put in the hands of a court appointed Receiver. He did not appoint a Receiver for any other Oyston assets and was willing to let Owen Oyston sell those as he wanted. In that courtroom he made it clear that he had reached this decision because it was evident that allowing Owen Oyston to continue as the owner of Blackpool FC would jeopardise its very existence. The actions taken by so many Blackpool fans over a long and sustained period proved that leaving the club in Oyston ownership was not an option. It is now a matter of court record that whilst the legal actions brought by Valeri Belokon against Owen and Karl Oyston and Blackpool FC provided the opportunity for a change of ownership and inflicted massive financial penalties on them, it was the fan boycott – "The most brilliantly orchestrated campaign in football" (quote from The Guardian newspaper) – that ensured the removal of the Oystons, once and for all.

At the homecoming game on 9th March 2019, when Bloomfield Road was packed to capacity in celebration of the first Oyston-free home game, the names of Seasiders who had passed away during the years of the boycott were read out. There were over 200 people who had made the agonising decision to stay away from their beloved football club who did not live to see our return. They paid the biggest price of all.'

The supporters won the club back. A football club is nothing without its fans, and Blackpool fans proved that.

The Supporters

'The darkness hides the empty places in the ground, not that there are many. Packed together, flat caps aplenty, cigarette smoke clouding the vision, the floodlights penetrate the gloom and enlighten the lush green turf. He turns to his friend and smiles. This is going to be a good night, and at that moment the team run out on to the pitch, resplendent in their blue-striped shirts. A roar follows. The bright colours explode in the grey gloom, and yes there's Hampson, hands on hips, bristling as he stares at the defenders before him.

The young boy is at the back of the Kop. It is full, the tangerine on the right, the others on the left. He has made it without incident, but he knows it will be a different story after the game. The noise is deafening, and he watches as the tangerine shirts jog up and down, flexing their muscles. Tony Green runs down the right of the pitch in fits and bursts of energy and Jimmy Armfield speaks quietly to those around him. The young boy was told by his father that this was the place where Matthews and Mortensen and Mudie ran teams ragged, but that was a different time. He closes his eyes and sees the maestro dribbling this way and that, his immaculate tangerine shirt rippling in the breeze left by his leopard-like movements.

The old man takes his seat and remembers the same time, except he had been there. He had watched as 'Morty' scored bullet-headed goals that made the netting shake with anger. He had watched as Mickey Walsh had thundered a ball into the Sunderland goal that rocked the television gantry, and he had seen the brief glory as Charlie Adam had splayed passes across a pitch that was his calling in life. Now he looks around at the empty seats, the cold wind blowing scraps of rubbish across the brown, marked pitch and only sees the tangerine that connects this world to the last...'

All football fans are essentially the same. They all love their clubs with an unreasoned passion, and at times an obsession. The rivalry with other clubs' supporters can be unhealthy, almost irrational with its hatred aimed at another human being who wears different colours. Other times it can be a force for good, uniting a community and giving pleasure when there is little to be found elsewhere. In the dark days of a war, a depression, a personal crisis, the walk to a football ground can suddenly lift the spirit, quicken the step, make the heart beat a little faster. It is a recreation and a life all rolled into one.

Blackpool fans are not unique. They are like the supporters of virtually every other club in the world, but what they did was unique. They collectively made a decision to do the one thing that was the most difficult, and they stuck to that decision. They boycotted home games at Bloomfield Road for a period of time whilst the deeply unpopular Oyston family continued to own the club, and they refused to break that boycott under all kinds of threats and temptations. Not all. Some continued to attend, giving the excuse that it was what they always did, but they did it with their heads bowed, sneaking through the turnstiles with collars turned up and hats lowered, covering their eyes. It caused a divide, one that may take a long time to be healed, but ultimately the boycotters won, and the fans are now united again. Mostly.

I wonder what William Blundell would have made of it if he were still alive? He was born in 1880 and started watching Blackpool when he was eight years old, just 12 months after their formation. Can you imagine the difference he would see if he were miraculously transported to the 21st century from his usual position at the entrance to the white-roped ground called 'Raikes Hall'? He would stand there and wait for the players and offer to carry their kit. If one of them agreed, then it was free admission to the ground, or else the unavoidable wait until half-time when the gates were unlocked. He apparently watched Blackpool right up to his death in the 1970s, which is a lifetime of memories, of triumph and defeat, of good days and bad.

He watched Blackpool's first ever goalkeeper, Alan 'Lal' Wright, who wore a cap to cover his bald patch. He saw Harry Bedford play, at the time one of the top strikers in the country with 118 goals in 180 appearances for the club. Bedford didn't do much running, it seems, but he knew where to be when the ball was crossed. Mr Blundell saw the great Jimmy Hampson and presumably cried like all other grown men at the news of his death, and then he watched as the Joe Smith era brought the incredible success that has defined the club since. He presumably saw the decline, too, but was able to delight in the talents of Green, Ball and Charnley.

There is no record of William Blundell ever being in trouble whilst following the team, but many Blackpool fans have. As early as 4th November 1905 the unruly element amongst a crowd of 2,500 made the headlines (or what were regarded as newspaper headlines in those days).

During a 3-0 home defeat to a superior West Bromwich Albion side, the referee had made some rather controversial decisions. One of them was actually sending a Blackpool supporter from the ground for unruly language, and another was sending off a Blackpool player (which made a little more sense). Sadly, it didn't endear him to the supporters who at that time were watching a team firmly at the wrong end of the table, and so as two burly policemen escorted the hapless official off the pitch at full time, around 200 fans invaded in a threatening manner. The club was severely censured afterwards by the Football League – and so the 'Blackpool hooligan' was born, long before anyone knew what that was. No one was wearing red-and-white scarves tied to their wrists and there weren't any replica shirts around, but the passion and sense of injustice was as tangible then as now.

They were at it again in 1919, on 24th May to be exact. A semi-final defeat to Liverpool by a single goal in the Lancashire Senior Cup, and the poor referee was again escorted from the pitch following a full-time invasion. The supporters were so starved of any kind of success after nearly a quarter of a century that any type of loss from a promising position was seen as the fates conspiring against them. Then, as now…

Let us take a moment top look at the 'average' Blackpool supporter in those days of the 20th century. I use the word 'supporter' because although 'fan' was first used in the USA at the end of the 19th century, its popularity was some way away in the UK. By 1925, a quarter of the way into the century, Blackpool had done nothing, absolutely nothing (unless you include an FA Cup win at mighty Sheffield United in 1906, or a couple of fourth-place finishes in Division Two), and attendances used to hover between 5,000 and 10,000 with the occasional higher figure depending on the visitors. Bloomfield Road was functional, with four sides and a relative amount of comfort for the day. There was even the new Blackpool Supporters' Club which had started in 1924, boasting 300 members, so the club was moving along slowly, under its own steam, not really bothering anyone. The problem was, there were far more important things than a football club to care about.

If you were an adult around in the mid 1920s, you had already survived a World War. It is possible that you had lost members of your family, friends, lovers or neighbours. Even some of the players who had turned out in a

Blackpool shirt (normally coloured red, black and yellow during the war in deference to the number of Belgian soldiers stationed in the town) may have gone missing. Real life was too serious to worry too much about the football team. In Blackpool, people were still being fined for cycling on the pavement, but you could take solace in the fact that there were 13 cinemas in the town for entertainment, the radio was becoming popular and church attendance on a Sunday was almost obligatory. Afterwards, you could take a stroll at the newly designed Stanley Park. Oh, and if you were struggling for money, you could always sell your teeth to a business called 'Myers Watch Shop' on Talbot Road. What happened to those teeth afterwards is something I have decided not to pursue.

Blackpool Football Club was not really that important, even to the people of the town. Bloomfield Road didn't even have a sign on it to denote it belonged to the football club. If 1925 was to be defined by anything, it was that the players complained of not being able to see each other in an FA Cup game at Blackburn Rovers as the orange and black shirts seemed to get lost in the fog. A 1-0 defeat in front of over 60,000 spectators was actually quite impressive. Major Frank Buckley was the disciplinarian manager and top scorer Harry Bedford was just about to be sold to Derby County for an incredible £3,000 fee.

1925 was an unremarkable year for the Blackpool supporter, except they were able to see the building of a new terrace at the southern end of the ground. It meant the capacity was now 20,000, but there weren't 20,000 Blackpool fans at that point. It housed the new boardroom and trophy cabinet but there was nothing to put in the latter. The directors got themselves a place in the corner stand away from the smoke of the steam trains that passed by, of which *Gazette & Herald* reporter Ernest Lawson wrote, *'It's a nice box they have placed themselves in, it must be for safety, for it is far enough out of the way. But of what are they frightened?'* It could have been the discontented supporters, but more than likely the sparks from the passing trains.

Syd Bevers' 'Atomic Boys' were two decades away, and the second quarter of the century was to see major change, yet within five years the club was in the First Division. It was 30th August 1930. It was FA Cup winners Arsenal. It was a new era for Blackpool.

'I was so nervous. I remember that. It was as if it were me who was

playing, you know? I had a cuppa in the morning and a piece of toast and got me coat on and ran for the tram. There were others there as well and I think we all felt the same. Billy jumped on and shook me hand and sat next to me. He gave me a ciggie and we just sat and smoked waiting for the stop.

I'd not seen the new terrace. I live in Fleetwood, you see, so going to Blackpool wasn't something I did unless it were necessary, so as I walked along from the prom, I saw this huge structure and there were people stood right at the top. It looked enormous and gave the ground a really odd look, slightly unbalanced if you will. I said to Billy, 'What do you think?' and he just smiled, so we ran the last 20 yards or so and got in the queue. I've never seen so many there before. We paid our sixpence and then we had to walk up these stairs that seemed to be stretching to heaven. Once we got to the top the view was fantastic. The ground looked so different, and it was already nearly full. There was this murmuring and excitement that I hadn't heard before. Billy reckoned it'd be a good idea just to stand where we was and watch from there. I'm too old for all that swaying around.

Anyway, we stood at the top. It were a bit chilly up there with the wind, but the view was great. Blackpool had put on a grand show. Brass bands and some Arsenal lads carrying the cup on a table around the ground. We waved our caps in the air, but I couldn't really understand why they thought we'd be interested. It's not our cup is it? Maybe one day. We saw the Mayor and his lady wife, and they stood and said something into a microphone, but no one could hear what they were saying where we were.

'How many do you think?' Billy shouted to me, and I said 'about 30,000' but I didn't really know because I'd never seen so many here before.

'No, yer daft clot. How many do you think they will score?' It were right funny. Anyway, we enjoyed the game but it weren't fun to watch. It's great being up here in the First but my, those Arsenal lads are good. Even Jimmy struggled to get the ball. I don't think we'll stand on that terrace every time. It's far too cold, and anyway I want to see what it looks like from somewhere else. We had a decent pint afterwards and back home. Blackpool bloody Football Club'.

The excitement of standing on a brand-new terrace (soon to be called the official Blackpool Kop) that held 12,000 spectators and was part of the highest crowd ever seen at Bloomfield Road, and for the first ever First Division game, must have been truly the most amazing moment.

There are images and grainy footage, but they can never convey the apprehension, the passion and the sheer enormity of it all. If you were a Blackpool fan in 1930, you were a witness to history.

The two World Wars saw Bloomfield Road essentially requisitioned by the RAF, so attending any competitive match was difficult as supplies and broken seats littered the stands, but at least it gave the local populace not on active duty a chance for some much-needed entertainment. Of course, victories over Huddersfield, Brentford and Wolves in 1939, leading up to the declaration of hostilities, meant that Blackpool topped the First Division, something that supporters clung on to proudly.

The town was substantially taken over by the Royal Air Force during the Second World War, with bed and breakfast hotels full of soldiers and medical units. There were strict blackouts, yet Hitler didn't seem too interested in bombing the seaside town as Blackpool was regarded as a good place for the Germans to visit after the invasion. Players and supporters bid their farewells, posted to faraway fields in France, and in many cases, never saw each other again.

Football continued to be played, admission prices stayed the same, but there was no programme to peruse before kick-off due to a lack of paper. There was little in the way of partisanship, as many who attended Bloomfield Road in those dark days had scant connection to the town they had been sent to, and as half of the ground was unusable (balanced by the £30,000 overdraft that was paid off by the armed forces) attendances always hovered around the 10/15,000 mark. No evening games. No lighting allowed, and fixtures called off at a moment's notice if an air-raid siren was heard. Dark days, indeed. Then again, there were far worse things taking place at that time.

Once the war was over, Britain was a grim and grey place. Although Blackpool had survived relatively unscathed, many towns and cities were peppered with vacant bomb sites, unrepaired buildings, prefab houses and allotments springing up from gardens. Rationing was extensive, and although bread was freely available, butter, tea and coal were difficult to acquire. The military dominated, with four times as many armed personnel as today, second only to the United States in its size. Stress amongst the civilian population was higher than realised following the horrors of war, but employment was by and large available. Flat-capped men were the labourers, white-collared types were in the office dictating to the labourers.

It was grey and damp. Grey because of the soot that clung to buildings and stained clothes. Open fire heating was the normal in those days and the smoke that came from the thousands of chimneys was not only polluting and dangerous to health but mingled with the constant rain until smog became a factor. London suffered a five-day smog that kept people at home and the capital bathed in an unearthly haze.

Entertainment was high among people's priorities. Anything to escape the depression of a victorious country attempting to get back on its feet, and of course the sporting grounds were where the majority of the male population found an escape, even if the female interest was comparatively low at that time. Football played its part and terraced grounds, rebuilt or hastily repaired, were crammed with thousands of spectators. Bloomfield Road saw its highest attendance, 38,098 against Wolves in 1955, never to be matched again, whereas crowds of 60,000 up and down the country were commonplace. There was passion and commitment from the fans. For instance, a Mr Joe Wade cycled to north London for Blackpool's FA Cup quarter-final with Arsenal in 1953, and I assume he cycled back, too. Why he chose to do that is something I have struggled to find out, but hey, what a weekend he had! It was all so grey, though.

This is of course the moment that Syd Bevers and the 'Atomic Boys' came in. There can't be too many Blackpool fans who haven't heard of him and the seriously crazy antics he and his gang got up to in that era? The duck painted tangerine that was released on to the pitch before kick-off (can you imagine that happening today?), and that weird costumes they wore? Well, here is a bit of a recap, as told by the man himself. Firstly, why on earth they decided to do it.

'It was a marathon match with Middlesbrough (Elland Road, 4th February 1946). We had drawn the two-legged FA Cup tie 5-5 on aggregate and had

to play a deciding game at a neutral ground and Leeds was selected. At that game I particularly noticed there was something missing in an England that was recovering from the Second World War and needed something to brighten up spirits generally. And that was colour. I don't think you'd have known who was supporting who – there was definitely a distinct lack of colour.'

Can you imagine a lack of colour at a football match? This was post-war England, though. As with all defining moments that involve Blackpool and a change off the pitch, they lost the game 1-0. No matter. Syd went to work and immediately called up his fellow fans and somehow persuaded them to lose their minds once a week as they followed the club. They called themselves 'The Atomic Boys' because the word atomic was popular at that time. Britain had just become the world's third nuclear nation after detonating a bomb off the coast of Australia, and so it was the 'word of the moment' – plus, as Syd said, 'they went down a storm wherever they went'.

The original costumes were obviously going to be tangerine coats with white trousers, but Syd decided it was too samey, so the rest of the gang just wore what they wanted. They attracted attention (inevitably) and became a draw when Blackpool and Matthews were in town. Actually, Blackpool were one of the biggest attractions when they played, either because it would be a trip to the seaside, or because of the crazy followers carrying a duck with them.

There were three ducks. Donald (what else?), Douglas (presented by Douglas Fairbanks Jr after a premiere of his film, *Mr Drake's Duck*) and Puskas (named after the player). They were initially white, as many ducks are, but the idea of dying them tangerine was probably one that wasn't quite thought through.

'We thought it would be simple. We acquired some finny haddock dye from another friend, filled the bath with water, mixed the dye in and we were ready for action.' The duck was duly taken to the bathroom and put into the tangerine-coloured water. 'But what we did not expect was the act that followed. The duck panicked, flapped its wings all over the place and the whole of the bathroom, plus us, were covered in tangerine dye. What a mess to clean up!'

Thereafter, perhaps not surprisingly, the ducks remained white.

One of the ducks – and I don't know which one as maybe the other two had died of fright – was smuggled into Wembley for the '53 Cup final. It was against the advice of Stanley Matthews (who seemed to be quite sensible about these things), but Syd hid him under his coat and, each time it made a noise, he would cough as cover. The night before, he had turned up at 10 Downing Street to present a stick of rock to the Prime Minister, Winston Churchill, but he wasn't at home. It was reported by the London press as a scene that involved men 'as gay as a pack of clowns in a harlequinade'. This was 1953.

The 'Atomic Boys' were of their era, yet somehow survived until the 1960s. Blackpool's decline and the arrival of a new type of supporter meant that old men wearing Egyptian outfits with straw hats carrying a dyed duck weren't exactly entertaining any more. Syd tried to revive the old gang for the 1980 season when Alan Ball was manager, but as he said in an understatement, 'It was doomed to failure.' The football fan was changing.

It might be interesting to also be aware of the *number* of Blackpool supporters who travelled to Wembley for the three FA Cup finals. Despite the old stadium comfortably holding 100,000 fans, mostly stood in the open air, finalists were only given an allocation of 12,000 tickets each. In 1953 that was increased to 13,000, so the majority of the fans of Blackpool, Manchester United, Newcastle United and Bolton Wanderers were left at home listening to the crackly radio commentary or the first black-and-white, grainy images on their underpowered television box. One Blackpool fan was there in 1953, though. George Mane. He sat in the main stand in one of the most expensive seats, paying nearly ten shillings for the privilege.

There was no noise. Just a silent buzz around the stadium. It was hard to believe that there were 100,000 there. It was almost like the Bolton supporters were embarrassed, ashamed to be denying Stanley again. Three rows in front of him were the two old ladies and a young man, blue-and-white rosettes and a blue-and-white striped knitted hat on one of their heads. They had whooped for joy when the third went in, stood up and applauded and cheered when the hobbled Eric Bell headed past Farm, but now they were sat in silence. All the other Trotters were too. They felt guilty. They felt like they were ruining the party. The Cup was theirs, but no one else wanted them to have it.

George glanced up at the clock, the sun's weak rays temporarily glinting in his eye, and saw the hand move almost imperceptibly to twenty-five past four. 'There's only 20 minutes,' he said to no one in particular, but there was no reply.

'Play up lads,' came a cry behind him. 'It's not over yet you know...' It was, though. It was over again.

Billy, sat next to him, pulled out a cigarette and offered it to George, but George just shook his head and turned back to the pitch. Billy didn't say much at the best of times. He wasn't saying much now. He watched as George Farm in the distance looked like he was shouting, but there was nobody close. 'He's probably shouting at himself,' he thought. 'He's had a right stinker of a game.' He looked and saw Johnston in the centre of the pitch, clapping his hands and urging on the team. Only 'Morty' looked interested. Where was Matthews? Isn't this all about him? Isn't this the day he finally wins that medal? Isn't the Queen here just to see him? What is he doing? Nowt, that's what. Hardly seen him touch the ball.

'Come on Trotters,' the older lady shouted in a high staccato voice. It wasn't needed though. They were coasting. Three finals and three losses, eh? Bloody Blackpool.

Then there was a roar from the other side of the stadium, people in the seats standing up, those that stood craning their necks and bobbing up and down. What was happening? It was Stanley galloping down the right wing like a gazelle, passing Banks and then floating the ball into the area. Where did that come from? Has he just realised what the score is?

George watched as the brown ball seemed to hover, and as he stood up to get a clearer view, the Bolton keeper Hanson missed it, and Morty was there to put it away.

Goal!!

'By heck George. We're back in it,' shouted Billy as he waved his hat in the air. 'What about that eh, lasses?' looking down at the Trotters who didn't move. It was 3-2. Still time.

'I'll have that ciggie now...'

On the pitch the tangerine shirts, glistening in the sunlight, seemed to be everywhere. They were at the back, they were in the middle, they were at the front. In the haziness of the day, George could see Joe Smith stood at the edge of the pitch, hands in pockets, his heavy dark suit giving him the impression of a gangster. He was saying nothing, but he was staring. He was watching. He was looking. If they still lose this, what will he say to Matthews and to Mortensen and to Johnston and to Mudie? Then he made a gesture. George couldn't see what it was exactly, but he saw Mudie nod his head and run to Perry. They spoke briefly and then they switched wings.

'What's he doing, Billy?' shouted George as the crowd began to murmur again, but Billy had no idea. 'It might work.' It did.

It didn't at first. George, buoyed by the goal, fidgeted in his seat. It wasn't the same, sat down watching the football, but they'd agreed that this was probably the last time 'Our Stan' would get a chance for a medal, so they paid a King's ransom and bought the tickets. Now he wished he was behind the goal with the lads who were waving their caps and shouting at the team. You couldn't do that here.

Blackpool kept going forward in waves. The Bolton lads were on their knees. Tired, dejected, despairing, but they were still winning. What's wrong with them? He looked at the Trotters sat below him, and they were ashen faced. The older lady was biting her nails, her fingers trembling. The younger one was talking to the lad, but it was forced. Something was happening, but it had to happen fast. A corner. A clearance. Another minute gone.

'It's done, George. Look at the clock.'

The clock said 4.44. It was the last minute. No more. He looked at Joe Smith. He was still stood with his hands in his pockets and was staring. He hadn't moved. Then the crowd roared again.

'Free kick, George. This is it.'

Then there was a hush. The Bolton defenders lined up a wall and the keeper was trying to shield his eyes. Matthews stood at the far of the pitch, removed and waiting. Morty stood over the ball.

'I can't look…'

'You have to look. For the boys. For Stan. You have to…'

Then it was done. Morty waving his arms in the air, Perry jumping around and Stanley running to his captain and hugging him. The Blackpool fans jumping and leaping and hugging, their rosettes and homemade scarves creating a jamboree of tangerine. The stadium was electric, and the loudspeaker announced that it was the first final hat-trick in the history of the Cup. Even the Queen seemed to smile, but she always did. It was 3-3. Not all over, after all.

Down below, the Bolton lady started crying. George wanted to hold her, but he was too excited. The Trotters around the stadium looked at their team and seemed to guess. There was no time for anything else, surely? What happens if it's a draw? It's never happened before…

'Go on, Blackpool…' as Matthews finds a run down the right, but his crossed ball is booted away. 'Go on, lads.'

George looked at the clock. It was on 46. It must be finished. Then he looked at Stanley. He was running again, weaving this way and that. Why hasn't he done this all the game? He beats his defender. Don't know which one. It doesn't matter. He beats him. He's at the byline. Cross it Stan, cross it! He crosses it. It takes forever, but he gets the ball into the area, the Bolton players stumbling and staggering to protect their goal, but it's too late for them. There's Perry. The ball. His foot. The goal….

George doesn't remember much after that. He cried. He shouted. He hugged. He swore. He apologised to the old lady, who just smiled and walked away. Billy got out a hip flask and drank the brandy he'd saved for the occasion, letting George have a hefty swig. Neither of them could really see the Cup being presented by the Queen or Johnston lifting it high. They saw Matthews though, shoulder high on his team-mates, a smile as wide as the Channel on his face. He heard announcements over the loudspeakers but couldn't remember a single one of them. He watched as the stadium emptied, apart from the Blackpool fans who crowded at the pitch wall to get closer. Even though there were 13,000 of them, they seemed to be lost in the expanse of the stands. There was a chant of 'Yes we have no bananas' and he saw good old Syd Bevers run on to the pitch and hug George Farm. Blackpool had won the Cup. Matthews had his medal. Morty had scored a hat-trick, and we'd all seen the beautiful Queen Elizabeth II. What a day...

Nothing was the same after that. The fans of the 1950s had had their day. Their day in the sunshine. Their day when they could boast at work that they'd won the bloody Cup. They had the parade on the promenade, a white 'Seagull' bus edging its way through the crowds, dark-suited players smoking cigarettes and smiling wide, with the Cup at the front, looking like it was about to topple over. They craned their necks to get a glimpse of Stanley as he stood on the Town Hall steps and listened as they heard him say it was about eleven players and not just him, but they knew it wasn't true. Even Morty said it was 'for Stanley', and he'd scored three times. They saw Joe Smith, smiles and laughter, and the Mayor, in all of his regalia, hand over the specially engraved cigarette lighters to each player. The radio men were there, the newspaper men and photographers and even the television camera, bulky and obstructing, but it was expected. Most of them didn't return for a very long time. By the time the 1960s arrived, Blackpool Football Club was a footnote in history. The fans, dwindling in numbers, tried to imagine a new era of success, but it was slipping away.

The 1960s was supposed to be a carefree and fun-loving time, but that really only applied to London, where Carnaby Street and hippy power and recreational drugs were what the youngsters enjoyed. Elsewhere in the country, well it was just a case of leaving the dark tunnel of the post-war 1950s into the bright and sunlit era of the 1960s. Popular music, started in America, was now being given a British accent with the Beatles, the

Rolling Stones and the Who, to name but three. Fashions changed. Still, a sombre suit was worn to the office (complete with John Steed bowler hat and cane), but the younger generation found that a smart jacket and thin tie worked wonders. That was just the men. The females came alive with the mini-skirt, knee-length boots and bright-painted lips, and so the dynamic of the football supporter changed too.

Bloomfield Road was gradually emptying. From the packed houses of the previous decade to the sight of concrete terraced steps clearly visible amongst the spartan crowds, it was the top of the slippery slope. Attendances had kept at a respectable number as the new decade dawned, but as the years passed, the 30,000 dropped to 25,000, which in turn fell to 20,000 and then soon hovered between 10,000 and 15,000. Blackpool were no longer an attraction. Bloomfield Road no longer a place to tell tall tales about. Having said that, standing on the Kop on a glorious sunny day, with the inadequate roof above, was still a pleasure. It was busy, but it was comfortable. You could move around, not hampered by close bodies and rain-sodden macs. It was a time when a new type of supporter arrived, the young ones who liked to sing. Inspired by the 'proper' Kop at Liverpool (who seemed to sing Beatles songs throughout the game and little else), the Blackpool lads came out with their own hymns.

'2, 4, 6, 8, who do we appreciate? B. L. A. C. K. P. O. O. L. Blackpool!'
'La la la, Leslie Lea…'

It was innocence. It was a time before the hooligan and the switchblade and the bovver boots. It was fun, even if watching Blackpool wasn't always. By the time the 1960s started to fade away, with the black jackets, white shirt and black tie replaced by the wide collar, platform shoes and Oxford bags, the atmosphere on the terraces had started to change too. Many of the older supporters of today were introduced to the club at this time. Missing the delights of Matthews, Mortensen and Mudie by a few years, they were seduced by the dazzling shirts of Green, Ball and

Charnley. Alban O'Brien (Terminally Tangerine) fell in love with the team at this stage:

'The first match I can remember was against Liverpool and, in those days, there was a fashion for sticking balloons on the middle of the pitch. I can remember running on and popping the Liverpool balloons and putting tangerine ones in their place. As for many people, it was the 1966 World Cup that lit my fire and the fact that, at least during the duration of the competition, England's fireball and tireless engine at the heart of the team was our player. I am sure, though I wouldn't admit it, when Tony Parr read out the dedication to Alan Ball at BR years later, I was moved to tears... Perhaps the first signing I can remember was Gordon Milne who came in 1967, but the great Alan Skirton must have arrived the year before. After that, I was hooked...'

Peter Seddon, lifelong fan, remembers his indoctrination in the 1960s:

'Being a football fan is all about routine and superstition. As a youngster back in the 1960s, Saturday home games were always the same – at 12 noon I would be dispatched to the Lane Ends Chippy on Hawes Side Lane with a bag, large dish, list and a 'ten bob' note – three steak puddings with lashings of gravy, a fish, two huge portions of chips and three lots of peas! I remember it as if it was yesterday. By 1.15pm it was time for Dad and me to walk round to meet with my dad's mate Brian and his son Christopher and off we toddled down to Bloomfield Road, full of expectation or dread – usually both! We had to go that early because of the size of the crowds – particularly when it was Liverpool, Everton or Manchester United – and if we wanted to get 'our spot' on the wall over on the west side of the Kop (Dad and Brian went towards the back with all the 'blokes') we needed to be there by 2pm latest. Memories of a sea of heads, the smoke of countless cigarettes and the noise! It became my fix at a very early stage of my life. This was Saturday, week in, week out when 'Pool were at home. Being ten years old in 1966, I remember migrating down towards the front of the Kop in the days of Tony Waiters – who seemed like a colossus to me, a huge heroic figure. He used to wear a flat cap just like my dad's, too! Although we'd lost Emlyn Hughes to Liverpool, we still had 'Bally' at that time and, when he got the ball, there was expectation and excitement on another level. It wasn't like opening Xmas presents excitement, this was something you felt in your soul, initiating that indefinable 'thing' that becomes part of a football fan's DNA.

Once experienced, it is in you forever. For me it became part of who I am, dominating my life to a ridiculous degree – cut me and I bleed Tangerine.'

The bridge between the 1960s and the 1970s was built at Deepdale, Preston. On Monday 13th April 1970, the transition between the old Blackpool fan to the new Blackpool fan took place. From the flat-capped, Woodbine-smoking, sodden-raincoated working man, to the tangerine-scarved, youthful and abrasive skinhead. It was the night at Preston where innocence and charm were replaced by obsession and abrasiveness. It wasn't that anything untoward actually took place on that famous evening, but it was the start of a rivalry that soon transcended football and reached out to other clubs with their own loyalties.

At a time when attendance figures meant little and segregated sections were unheard of, it was estimated that over 20,000 Blackpool fans travelled along the A583 (pre-M55 days) or caught the train or bus for the fixture with Preston. It was also at a time when there was no rivalry between the clubs or the supporters, with some enjoying the delights of Bloomfield Road and Deepdale every other weekend. The crowd was unofficially 34,000, but most of it was swathed in tangerine, and of course every self-respecting Blackpool fan knows that Fred Pickering scored a hat-trick to give them promotion to the First Division, effectively sending Preston North End to Division Three (they actually saved that embarrassment for the following weekend, but Blackpool had made their survival almost impossible). After the game, the Blackpool fans celebrated in style, whilst the Preston fans slunk back to their homes, satisfied that the humiliation was over. There was no sign of any type of trouble. Jimmy Armfield commented many years later that he felt that was the night the rivalry between the two sets of supporters began, and it's interesting to remember that in the next two 'derby' League fixtures at Deepdale in 1972 and 1973 (big wins for Blackpool on both occasions), the atmosphere was tenser and very unpleasant. Blackpool fans, with their scarves tied to their wrists, Doc Marten boots and Northern Soul tops, overwhelmed the Preston supporters, who had yet to experience the ravages of hooliganism that had now blighted the seaside town like few others.

'1970 was a watershed moment – Deepdale, the Fred Pickering hat-trick hammering of 'them up the road' to effectively promote us and relegate them. How sweet could football be?! My main memories of that day were

of travelling with my mate and his dad in their car, and from Blackpool to Preston it was just a sea of Blackpool fans. At the ground we paid on the turnstile at the Town End thinking that was where all the Seasiders would be, but it was obvious that we were everywhere, including on the cinder track. We decided to go round to the Kop, and I will never forget as long as I live the sight of my pal's dad – dressed as dads did back then with shirt, tie and jacket – in the middle of a tangerine multitude being bounced up and down on those wooden sleepers to the tune of 'Knees up Mother Brown'...'
(Peter Seddon)

If Bloomfield Road mirrored the state of football in the nation, then it had become a dangerous place to spend a Saturday afternoon. Blackpool fans, once regarded as passive and welcoming, now felt the need to guard the 12,000-capacity terraced Kop from the onslaught of larger numbers who were attracted to the town and its cheap entertainment. I vividly remember standing at the top and looking behind as thousands of blue-

and-white scarved West Brom fans arrived, knowing that this was going to be 90 minutes where the football was just a distraction. Walking up the steps at the back of the Kop to see hundreds of Chelsea supporters in the section where we normally stood was a first, too. Outside, the derelict railway site, broken bricks, steel sleepers and stones, was a perfect place for the hooligan-minded to ply his (or her) trade. Also, outside the ground, painted on the wall of the East Stand, were the words 'I want to knife a Preston bastard'. Football had changed, and Bloomfield Road had changed with it.

By the mid '70s, hooliganism was out of control, and Bloomfield Road saw the first murder at a football game in England. On 24th August 1974, Kevin Olsson was stabbed to death during a skirmish with Bolton Wanderers fans, his murderer never found. Afterwards, the Sports

Minister Dennis Howell visited the site and Blackpool introduced steel fencing to separate the two sets of opposing fans. It made little difference, as the hooligans took their entertainment outside the ground after the game. The police, heavily backed up by Black Marias, seemed unable to cope. Despite this, Bloomfield Road still hosted decent attendances and the Blackpool fan was still able to wear his (or her) tangerine scarf and bobble hat with pride.

'They're coming.

I'm staying.

Mate, there's too many of them. We can't cope.

I'm staying.

I stayed and he left. I stayed and I watched as Mickey Walsh took the ball to the right of the pitch. It was the 87th minute and he had the confidence. I watched as he shimmied to the left and then unleashed a thunderbolt that was inch perfect and moved at an unnatural speed into the Sunderland net. The ground erupted. The game was won. I didn't know it, but I'd just witnessed the goal of the season, forever etched in my future memory from a television angle. This would be the only time I'd see this version clearly.

They came. The rest was a blur. The game was won. The battle was overwhelmingly lost.'

The memories are still of a happier time.

At a time when away travel was still something of a novelty, *The Green* played a large part in the Saturday lives of Blackpool fans. Queuing up outside the newsagent at 5.15 waiting for the delivery van to arrive, and then the bundles of the green-coloured newspapers with the very latest from Blackpool's away game that afternoon. It has always amazed me how this paper, with the intricate first-half report and a few lines from the second, was published within half an hour of the game ending, especially with the technology of the time. *The Green* was then pored over with a cup of tea as League tables were studied intently.

For those who travelled to games via the non-motorway 1970s, it was an introduction to the comradeship of the time.

'*The Ozzie and Shep supporters' club buses were a revelation: long journeys, high spirits and the beer glass used as toilet as we drove around the centre of London, the regular stop-offs for a party at Walsall and Birmingham supporters' clubs on the way home, the getting lost in Shepherds Bush when they moved the coach, the skinhead gangs following us back to the coaches as we hid our scarves after the game, and trying to join in their chants in our best Brummie so that we wouldn't be recognised, the emptying of the Holte End at Villa and watching them approach like an army of claret-and-blue ants, and surround us on the away end... Hooliganism really was a problem...*' (Albon O'Brien)

By the time of the 1980s, the dynamic of the Blackpool fan had changed. The numbers were fewer and most of them just went because it was what they had always done. There was little attraction in attending football games at the crumbling Bloomfield Road, especially as the team had tumbled out of the top half of the Football League for the first time. There was no expectation, no belief that better times were just around the corner, and no delight in what they were witnessing on the pitch. They went, had a social gathering with friends they had seen for years, and then left. The team played, but mostly badly, and when Alan Ball made the comment that he felt the Blackpool fans had gone to the FA Cup tie with Fleetwood to see them lose, there was an element of truth in it.

For the Blackpool hooligan, the 1980s took on a more sinister tone. The proverbial big fish in a very small pond, the away following was larger than most clubs', and when Blackpool came to town, the locals knew it, albeit for the wrong reasons. A news report on the BBC, highlighting six of the worst hooligan mobs in English football, included Blackpool. After a night of mayhem in Torquay (surely just about the furthest a Blackpool fan could have travelled at that time), their reputation was sealed. In later years, TV presenter and Torquay United fan Helen Chamberlain said that 'Blackpool fans are mad'. A fixture that had been rearranged for a Saturday evening, so as to deter the travelling hooligan, Blackpool fans saw it as a challenge and turned up the night before. Two nights of mayhem and violence followed. Small towns such as Rochdale, Chester and Bury shuddered for years to come when the words 'Blackpool Football Club' were mentioned, as rampaging tangerine-scarved youths caused havoc, wearing shell suits and trainers with a switchblade in their pocket. Mark Hillary, a lifelong Blackpool fan, unashamedly recounts one occasion at Bury's Gigg Lane:

The evil that Blackpool fans do lives on… however, as someone once said, 'If you can remember the '80s you weren't there!' I was recently asked if I could recall that day and my abiding memory is more about being in Manchester before and after, but of course I do remember the Jericho moment when the walls came tumbling down! Like me, most of those boys will be almost pensioners now, but of course I don't get my old-age pension until I'm 66, so don't get me started!

There were a few away games around then; some local like Rochdale and Chester, but also further afield at Brighton and Gillingham, that I remember particularly where there must have been something in the sea air. To quote Helen Chamberlain (Sky Sports many years later) after another epic journey to Torquay in 1984; "Blackpool fans are mad".

My diary entry for that day (what, you haven't kept a diary for over 40 years? How weird are you?) says: "Bury (A) Train 8:00am – Lost 0-1 Robbery & riot. Met S later". As I say, my main memories of the day are being in Manchester before and after the Gigg gig and trying not to get involved with United and West Ham fans fighting all over the place. My good friend Gentleman Johnny got a few whacks from United mobs, but then he does sound a little bit cockney and United fans can recognise this as they speak like that, too.

My "Hit the Bar" colleague Neil Coupe, writing in February 1989, so a little more contemporaneous, said: "…the occasion being marred by structurally unsound perimeter walls and some unruly behaviour from the coast! Or was that the boys in blue!?" Bit disingenuous from Neil there, but I think as usual we can blame the referee. There is a lot online about the Rammy and Benny and organised trouble, but of the game I just remember feeling genuinely robbed near the end with a dodgy penalty for them. However, with penalties, my general rule is any penalty given against Blackpool is harsh and not sure 35 years of objectivity would change that.

A lot of disappointment, and I think the Blackpool fans in the wooden stand to our right started to pull the seats out and chuck them. Fans where I was on the covered terrace behind the goal made their way to the fences at the front and quite quickly to the one exit to the right and met the rather counter-productive tactic of keeping away fans locked in. Diverted to the brick wall next to the metal gate, they started to crush. I do remember thinking 'sod this' and climbing out through a turnstile, only to be pushed back in by a policeman. The walls were old and there was a real crush, and then some lads stood back and started to put shoulders to the task at hand. I heard no angelic trumpets but soon those walls started to move, the momentum and enthusiasm built and then came a tumbling down. On to a load of cars parked too close, as I recall. Not sure if they belonged to Pool fans but, anyway, I came on the train! It was then quite easy to get out through the now enlarged exit and go rampaging off into nice suburban Bury with the police having lost control.'

It was what Blackpool fans did and what they were good at. Unlike many other clubs though, the hooligan element grew up and didn't hand it down to a younger generation. Despite riot police being deployed in the game with Birmingham City at Bloomfield Road in 1989, that was more to do with the Blues than the Tangerines. By the time the decade came to an end, the ground was still decaying, the football was pretty dire, but it was a safer environment. Only occasionally in the years that followed and up to the present time, has Blackpool Football Club been connected to the worst excesses of fan violence. Even 'derby' fixtures against Preston and Burnley are relatively tame compared to the all-out war of earlier years.

Instead, the new and modern fan was able to start to take pride in their club, as Billy Ayre channelled that passion that exists in most supporters and turned it to the team's advantage. It is absolutely no coincidence that the incredible home run of form, that included 15 consecutive victories and 24 unbeaten matches, took place once Ayre had established his pre-match fist-clenching and arm-waving antics on the pitch. His 'showbiz' entry from the tunnel, running on to the turf and exhorting the fans to make as much noise as possible, intimidated the opposition and gave Bloomfield Road the reputation it has today, of a raucous and passionate crowd.

Blackpool fans were able to take this to a larger stage in 1991 and 1992 with the two Play-off finals at Wembley. 15,000 and 13,000 respectively (not the largest numbers, but larger than anything Blackpool had seen for quite some time) travelled to see the despair of Torquay United and the delight of Scunthorpe United. Attendances increased and the dark days started to become a distant memory. The fan of the 1990s still stood on too-low concrete terracing, bobbing this way and that to catch a

glimpse of the action behind other spectators, and they still had to wrap up heavily as the north wind blasted in their faces, but the whole thing seemed more fun. They could no longer stand on the Kop, but looking at the huddle of away supporters, shivering and normally wet on the roofless and seemingly abandoned terrace,

meant they were not really missing anything. With the far side of the East Paddock usually closed, Bloomfield Road was an odd place to follow your team, as the majority of home supporters were on the south side of the halfway line. If you ventured north in the West Stand, you would find enough space, but you were usually all alone. Blackpool fans didn't number many, but there was a passion amongst them that had not been seen since the early 1970s. Supporting Blackpool was something to be proud of again (despite the lack of success) and the new fad of replica shirts could be seen in Bloomfield Road and around the town.

'We used to live across the road from the training ground, so I'd go there with my scrapbook in the Billy Ayre days and ask them to sign it for me. Billy was lovely and always took time to come and speak to me. As I got older, I loved going to the games and got to know all the players from the training ground. Lee Martin and Phil Brown used to leave me and my dad tickets for the away games, and I got a few of Phil Brown's shirts. Everyone

Lifelong fan Leanne Smith when she was younger. She's already got Blackpool FC in her blood.

at school supported Man United or Liverpool, and I used to get a lot of grief for being a Blackpool fan, and being a girl, but the memories I have from the late '80s and early '90s I'll never forget.' (Leanne Smith – lifelong Blackpool fan)

The new century brought a new, rebuilt ground (eventually) and a crazy four-season spell where the team reached Wembley three times (or Cardiff's Millennium Stadium as it was called – actually used for Wembley in the film *28 Days Later*, as the new national stadium still wasn't complete). Leyton Orient in a Play-off final and Cambridge United and Southend United in the Football League Trophy final saw Blackpool as the most successful side in Wales – well, Cardiff anyway. 14,000, 13,000 and 16,000 fans travelled for the three games respectively, with the Southend match being the first time Blackpool fans had been outnumbered in a final. It mattered not, as they won all three games, regardless. Of course, it was the Cambridge game where former manager Billy Ayre was spotted in the crowd by Blackpool fans. His name was sung, and he was carried shoulder high. Blackpool supporters don't forget.

By 2007, with a charge to the Championship, the replica tangerine shirts could be seen in schools and on the streets and in the bars. Blackpool was cool again. Market stalls, once the preserve of Manchester United's red or Chelsea's blue, now sold Blackpool's tangerine, and the fact that this even has to be mentioned shows how low the club had fallen from favour down the years. Now with a couple of gleaming new stands at Bloomfield Road, the impressive car park where the old, disused railway tracks had been, and the professionalism that seemed to surround the club briefly, it was great to be a Blackpool fan. To that effect, 30,000 travelled to Wembley in

the pouring rain to see as dominant a performance as could be imagined in a Play-off final as Blackpool 'hammered' Yeovil Town 2-0. When Valeri Belokon stood on the pitch, tangerine tie waving in the wind, and announced he wanted the club in the Premier League within five years, we all just enjoyed the moment. Nothing could be better than what was happening. Championship football for the first time in 29 years. Bring on Preston and bring on Burnley, and yes let's listen to 'Glad All Over', which had somehow been nominated as the team's theme tune, despite it always belonging to Crystal Palace.

Three years later and of course a day that none of the 37,000 Blackpool fans present would ever forget. To see half of Wembley stadium, baking in a heatwave rarely seen or felt without discussing global warming, packed to the rafters with tangerine, was a sight that even today graces living room walls with framed photographs. The day, the excitement, the passion, the sheer ecstasy. Has there ever been a better day as a Blackpool fan? If the supporter who saw the first ever promotion at Boundary Park in 1929 could be transported forward in time by 81 years, would he or she agree it was better? The fans who watched Stanley Matthews in the same space 57 years previously, as he terrorised the Bolton defence in 20 final-defining minutes, would look at the colour of the stadium and

listen to the noise and wonder if they were living in the wrong Blackpool era. Was there a single Blackpool fan who didn't shed a tear or scream a profanity or say a silent 'thank you' to God as the final whistle was blown? How many slunk to the floor and put their head in their hands? How many stared, unbelieving, as Holloway ran on to the pitch and embraced Adam? How many thought of Manchester United, City, Chelsea, Arsenal, Liverpool? Every one of us did.

The emotions of the day. The memories. The knowledge that you had just witnessed history. 'Little Blackpool' (not as little as Wimbledon or Wigan or smaller than Burnley or Bolton) had made the 'Promised Land'. Wembley will never look the same. It will never resonate to the same sounds of hope and disbelief at the same time. No club, no matter who they are, will ever embrace the sheer force of willpower that the Blackpool fans had taken on as they roared on their team to the most unlikely of promotions. It will never be matched, never mind beaten.

It will be handed down to their children and to future generations. For the most emotional of stories, read this from Tim Sparks:

'Like any good, loving father, I gave my son little choice in who he would be supporting. Although his actual first game was at non-league Lancaster City where we lived when he was a few weeks old, he made his debut at Bloomfield Road at the age of four for a game against MK Dons in September 2005. He'd already named his first hero; Keigan Parker. It predominantly came from hearing me singing his name after scoring a winner at some away game that I didn't attend. 2-1 down at half-time with the wind howling and Parker on the bench, George was cold and bored, so his Mum took him to the arcades agreeing to meet me after the game. Sure enough, Parker came off the bench and Pool won 3-2. Lesson learned for George!

Over the years, his attendance at games was sporadic, never really getting the football bug, but he was always a Pool fan. As he grew, he also started to have issues with his development that culminated in him moving to a special school and requiring more and more help. His Mum and I separated which left me and George with less time, but more quality time together. Ian Holloway arrived in Blackpool and took us all on a whirlwind journey. As the season culminated, George was really starting to struggle physically and was prescribed a wheelchair to help him with fatigue. While he could still walk, run or dance, he tired so quickly and would frequently need carrying or would stumble. A trip to Wembley beckoned and for the first time in our lives, we attended as a wheelchair user and "carer". Like any other Pool fans, it was one of the best days of our lives. I hoped that George had enjoyed it as much as me, and when I looked back at the photos of the day, his grin after the game as we had a cuddle by the Bobby Moore statue told me everything I needed to know.

The Premier League beckoned and a trip to Bloomfield Road was arranged to buy George his first Pool shirt with the famous logos on the sleeves. By now he had developed a curious habit of declaring his favourite player to be whoever had "his number", ie. how old he was at the time. As we queued in the club shop discussions were had with other dads. "Who's he having on the back"? The replies pretty much ran between Adam &

Ormerod or something more personal. As we approached the front, I gave him one last chance. "George, are you absolutely sure? This might be your only ever Premier League shirt". His reply was instant – "Yes," he smiled, "My number". And so it was that I think he was possibly the only kid with "9 Harewood" on his back.

February came, and the Pool were defying all expectations and playing some fantastic football. Sadly, disaster struck. George was hit by a series of seizures that resulted in us both staying in Manchester Children's Hospital for a short time as nurses and doctors tried to stop them reoccurring. Things would never be the same again. The wheelchair was now permanent as we were advised that George had a rare, progressive life-limiting Mitochondrial disorder. He could no longer walk or feed himself and his speech became increasingly tricky to understand. One thing remained though – the grin! Over the next few years, he spent a lot of time in hospital, and in 2014 it was arranged for him to have a special day at Bloomfield Road as Pool took on Huddersfield Town. There were so many highlights, from meeting the players in the dressing room to lining up on the pitch as they came out for the game. But one man made the day for us. We had the honour of watching from the directors' box in the company of Sir Jimmy Armfield. He complimented George on his 'good English name' and asked us to wait for a photo while he did his hair after removing his cap! Throughout the game, Gentleman Jim lived up to his reputation, frequently asking me if George was okay and engaging with George. Even today, as I write this, I feel incredibly emotional at the memory. Today, as I write this, George is 19 and in good health, relatively speaking, and he's met more Pool players since the boycott ended. Most recently, Curtis Tilt showed genuine class to take extra time and effort with George at a 'meet the players' event, re-affirming George's love for the club, and increasingly shocking taste in favourite players!'

Of course, this story takes us beyond that crazy May day, but the inference is clear. You're a Blackpool fan, so your family will be too. Two years later and everything was different. Wembley was no longer basking in the sunshine and the Blackpool fans were completely outnumbered. Jaded by the prospect of another money-sapping visit to the capital and the prospect of disappointment, only around 29,000 made the journey. The West Ham United fans, with their 12-tube-stops journey to the national stadium, packed the stands with 46,000 fans, and it sounded like it too. 'I'm Forever Blowing Bubbles' over the loudspeaker, Trevor Brooking being interviewed on the pitch and Warren Mitchell walking around dressed in claret and blue, and you suddenly realised what the Cardiff fans had to endure two years previously. Add to that a referee less than attentive to fouls and an unusual lack of accuracy in front of goal, and the return back up the M6 was nowhere near as enjoyable. At least there wasn't the prospect of having to spend any more time with the population of East London, with their natural charm and wit. Then came the boycott.

Actually, as all Blackpool fans know, it didn't come immediately. Like the drip, drip, drip of a tap that refuses to be fixed, the water torture that was the Oyston empire gradually wore the fans down until action had to be taken. This is where the modern Blackpool fan can stand tall alongside their predecessors and say, 'We saved the club'. The supporter of the 1890s watched as the fledgling club came into being, stumbling its way through the obstacle course of the new game. The 1930s fan watched as the club started to reach maturity, with a football ground to be proud of and a hope of a grand future. The 1950s Blackpool supporter enjoyed the halcyon days of a well-prepared life, only for the 1980s fan to try and destroy its reputation. An Indian summer came for the fan in the early part of the 21st century, but the fan of the second decade was the one who kept the dying club alive. This was the fan who did more for the health and well-being of Blackpool Football Club than any other. This was the fan that was unique.

The protests hadn't worked. The walkouts, the demonstrations, the pitch invasions (of both tennis balls and human beings), even the funeral march all those years previously, hadn't budged the Oyston family. They sat there, defiant, grinning, almost taunting.

'We'll never sell the club,' came the cry from Karl Oyston. 'The protests are a busted flush.'

Blackpool fans didn't wince, didn't back down and didn't stop believing. Armed with the knowledge that Valeri Belokon was chasing his money through the law courts, and that football supporters up and down the country backed them (despite the seeming disinterest from the Football League), they went on the offensive. There was only one action now to take, and so the 'NOT A PENNY MORE' campaign began.

Three 'Judgement Days' had come and gone, each struggling slightly more than the last as Karl Oyston's words in 2014 were now failing in resonance. Travelling to watch non-League AFC Blackpool instead of  entering Bloomfield Road to watch the team play Leeds United hadn't worked, so it was simple. Cut off the family's lifeblood. Stop paying at the turnstile. Don't give them any more money. It would be tough, and it would tear families apart as some would continue to take a walk of shame and enter the ground, but the majority won. Empty seats, shown around the country by television cameras that had come to record a football match, but instead magnified a community movement, and Blackpool fans became famous the footballing world over. Even the League Two Play-off final at Wembley in 2017 against Exeter City was boycotted. Only around 5,000 fans travelled, of whom most were handed free tickets.

'The best trip' of the Premier League season had rocketed the tangerine-clad supporters to fame as they sang the song and waved their scarves in a riot of colour and passion, meaning each Premier League club's fans would enjoy the 90 minutes against Blackpool just that little bit more. Now those same fans were silent and absent. Even handing Bloomfield Road over to 8,000 Sunderland supporters (them again!) only delayed the inevitable. Something had to give, and it did.

When the Oyston family left the club, the whole town breathed a collective sigh of relief. It wasn't just because the club was now back in safe hands and the faded seats could now be covered by excitable football fans, it was the small businesses that had been affected due to the boycott. They could recover. The fans who had been chased through the courts and sued and fined, could now raise their heads and smile. The name of Blackpool Football Club, abused and abandoned for too long, could now be given a spit of polish and would soon be as good as new. Blackpool were back.

No Blackpool supporter who attended the 'homecoming' game

against Southend United in March 2019 will ever forget. The Twitter feed for the Southend local reporter said that he had never experienced an atmosphere quite like it, and that was before the game started. The stadium, so long ignored and unloved, now blossomed in the light of the bright tangerine that lit up the sky. The seats were full of some 16,000 ecstatic and excitable fans, the noise was effervescent and unceasing, and the game was unimportant. The injury-time equaliser was enough to keep the excitement at fever pitch for the rest of the weekend. Hardened sports reporters relayed the events via TV, radio and newspaper, fans from all over the country 'became Blackpool' again for that one day and the hope that change was going to come was realised as the weak sun gradually disappeared behind the Tower. Yes, Blackpool were back.

The Experience

Football matchday experiences are usually the same up and down the country. If you don't support West Bromwich Albion, then you probably have no idea what it's like at The Hawthorns. We support Blackpool, so we know what the feeling and atmosphere is like as we make our way to Bloomfield Road, but what was it like in the past? As each supporter made his or her way along the dusty track or the tarmacked road, or as they boarded the creaking electric bus or the gleaming double-decker, the rattling tram or the horse and cart, what was going through their minds as they waited to see Bedford, Hampson, Dodds, Matthews, Charnley, Suddick, Bamber, Adam and Spearing? What awaited them?

At the turn of the 20th century, there probably wasn't a matchday experience. Our lone voice from the past, William Blundell, gives us a glimpse of his as he waits for the players to arrive and begs them to let him carry their kit, so he gets free admission. Then what? Where does he stand? Next to the white rope that separates the spectators and the pitch? There won't be any pre-match entertainment or announcements over loudspeakers, and as watching football in his age was a relaxed affair, it's more than likely that people would just come and go, arriving midway through the game and leaving when they wanted to.

By the time the First World War had broken out, things were a little more organised, yet the Blackpool fan could still walk along the cobbled

Bloomfield Road uncertain whether a game would take place. War restrictions, a lack of players and the general privations of the conflict meant that watching football was a recreation, but an unimportant one. With the almost complete lack of private transport, the 1916 Blackpool supporter would probably have taken the electric tram, or even the horse and cart, to get him to the ground. A flask of tea and a jam sandwich stuffed in his coat pocket might be his only sustenance as refreshment kiosks weren't that regular. He may have a programme to read as he stood in the queue or waited on the terrace: Blackpool Football Club's first issue was printed in 1907 (although not too many during the war), but there would at least be a local newspaper that might give a few details.

By the 1920s and 1930s, the flat-capped supporter, walking along the Bloomfield Road in the greyness of the time, would be able to stop at the kiosk outside the ground and purchase a bag of chips and a hot drink. There would be programme sellers outside the turnstiles, something for him to read whilst he waited for the teams to come out. The Second World War would bring yet more challenges of course, with half of Bloomfield Road closed for the armed forces, and games being played as and when restrictions allowed. At least they were entertaining, and goals were plentiful.

The 1950s saw our fan accompanied more and more by his female partner as women's football was already popular in the United Kingdom and they were becoming more interested in the men's game. It meant for a less rowdy atmosphere as men tried to keep the swearing to a minimum.

'Ladies present. Mind yer words...'

'Oops, sorry miss. I was only jesting.'

The '50s saw the matchday experience extended by at least two hours, as that's how much earlier a fan would have to take his place in the ground, such was the size of the crowds at Bloomfield Road. In a ground that had a capacity of only 38,000, it was nearly always full in the days of Matthews and Morty. At least there was the programme to read and the antics of 'The Atomic Boys' to laugh at, as Syd raced across the pitch in his Arab costume chasing the startled duck. Such days.

The '60s were the last days of innocence as black-suited and sharp-tied young lads took their girls to the Kop and sang songs. It was good-natured and it was fun. Even the loudspeakers now played popular tunes before the game, meaning the sparse crowds could now sing along to the Beatles and Dusty Springfield. The football on offer wasn't as good as that ten years previously, but it was played in colour with the tangerine scarves replacing the grey flat caps.

From the '70s to the end of the century, the matchday experience could be a sinister one. The route from Blackpool North railway station to the ground could be hazardous as gangs of teenagers roamed around, all wearing different colours to tangerine, coming to the game looking for trouble. They found it as each young Blackpool fan rose to the challenge, the same as throughout the country. For those who wished for a footballing entertainment, it could be tainted by the antics on the vast Kop, or by the crude chanting aimed at opposing supporters. Football was now a mini war played out mostly in the streets of the town. Few older fans can forget the battles in the '70s against Chelsea, Sunderland (of course), Bolton and Preston, and in the '80s with the likes of Manchester City.

Now, in this modern age of football watching, the all-seated Bloomfield Road offers a modicum of comfort for the returning fans. A concourse with decent refreshment kiosks, a reasonably comfortable seat with access-all-areas viewing, and a roof that mostly keeps out the rain. The loudspeakers play music, and the half-time interval sometimes has local schoolchildren in a penalty shoot-out. The threat of violence has all but gone, but thankfully the passion of the fans is still there.

The man pulled his raincoat closer to his body and stepped off the bus. The rain was drizzling, the grey was darkening. In the distance, yellow-coloured car headlights illuminated the ground, the red painted words welcomed the devoted. He walked, his head down, the water soaking slowly into his hat. Alongside him walked others, some smoking, some talking in whispers, some agitated. There were queues at the turnstiles, and no one wanted to be the first to push his way to the front. It was orderly and calm, tense and excited. It was another day at Bloomfield Road.

Once inside, he looked up to the mass of humanity on the terracing opposite. Shoulder to shoulder, arm in arm, swaying and moving, they waited for their heroes. The air was full of smoke, the rain drizzled, and the brown ball lost itself in the gloom. He looked to his right and saw Hampson, jumping on his toes, stretching his legs, hands on waist, a steely glare to those around. His boots always looked too big, but those boots would see them through. A drop of rain fell into the man's eye, and he blinked it away. There was no way of reaching it with his hand as the crowd closed in and crushed him so that the warmth of the bodies beat the winter's cold.

Looking again, he saw Johnston talking to Matthews. The tangerine shirts were already stained darker as the rain soaked the material. They'll be heavy to play in today. Matthews nodded and pointed to Morty, who stood on the centre spot, right foot on the ball, waiting for the signal to start. Joe Smith took his seat, his eyes level with the pitch. He was smiling, but then he always smiled.

Suddenly there was a collective roar of laughter and he saw the duck, painted crudely in orange and white, being chased theatrically down the pitch by Syd, his Arabian costume flapping behind him. The rain had stopped, and a smell of Bovril overwhelmed the man. He closed his eyes and savoured it, for once cursing at the popularity of this place, meaning he wouldn't be able to get to the kiosk until half-time at least. His stomach rumbled and he reached for a cigarette to take away the pangs.

'Come on lads, let's do it…'. It was the unmistakably squeaky voice of Alan Ball. Ginger hair as bright as his shirt, waving his arms like a windmill, a bundle of energy. He won't be here for long, as the man looked at the opening gaps on the terraces, where once middle-aged men in their greyness bonded together in a common goal. Now that's all gone, and soon the best Blackpool player on the pitch will go with them.

'Calm down, lad. Let's do this properly…' was the response from Armfield, his number two shirt flapping gently in the wind. His captain's words were measured and firm. He'd seen so much, but wouldn't it be grand if Jim could win something here?

The sun shone and the man felt tired. The terrace was emptier now. People had gone and not returned. His coat was heavy, and he took it off, slinging it over his right arm. A smell of coffee and then the sound of the singing, if that's what it was called. The roof at the opposite end cast a shadow over the ones at the back swaying and pushing and insulting and threatening. Bill Bentley was tying his bootlaces, looking around him, ready for battle. Tommy Hutchison looked taller than ever, his lanky frame belying his talent. A young fan, scarf tied to his wrist, pushed past him without a word or an apology. This wasn't the Bloomfield Road he remembered. It was bright and colourful but it was tense, and it was unsettling. He shifted from one foot to the other, wondering if he should have paid an extra shilling for a seat, but he'd never sat down at a match in his life, and wasn't about to start now.

Somewhere in the distance there was a chorus of boos and he looked to see the manager, all suited and booted, walking along the touchline. The man wasn't popular, but it was hardly surprising. Suddenly he felt tired, so tired that he felt he couldn't stand much longer. Before he closed his eyes, he looked at the terrace opposite. It was roofless. It looked like a prison cage and it was virtually empty. Where did it all go?

The young boy sat in his seat, his new tangerine shirt worn proudly. In his hand was the picture he'd treasured for so long, and now signed by the man himself. He'd been scared about approaching him, especially as the game was only an hour away, but Charlie had grabbed the picture and scribbled his name and gave it back. He said something to the boy, but it was difficult to understand. He was sure it was something good. Now he sat next to his dad and waited for his tangerine heroes to take to the pitch. The ground was full, the crowd was singing, and the away fans were trying to compete. His stomach churned and he pulled his woollen cap down over his ears. This was always the best time of his week. This was the time he thought of time and again when he was at school. He turned to his dad and smiled.

'Take it all in, son,' his dad shouted above the noise. 'These are the memories you'll treasure forever.'

He nodded and closed his eyes briefly as the sun's rays caught them and he saw a flash. A flash of the future. It was his future. It was the future of everyone here. This was Bloomfield Road. This is Blackpool Football Club. He opened his eyes.

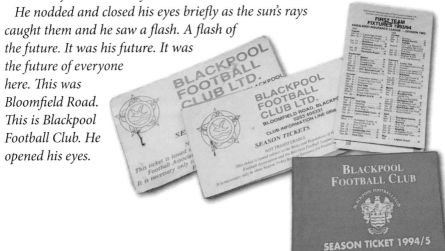

AUTHOR

Roy Calley saw his first Blackpool game in January of 1968 against Bristol City, and up to 1992 he was convinced he'd seen a 2-1 defeat. It was only when researching for the original *Complete Record* book that he found out that it was in fact a 1-1 draw, which shows that most Blackpool supporters see failure as inevitable.

Throughout the next 50-odd years, he has continued to follow the club through its many downs, as well as a few ups. Moving to the south of England and then to the south of France meant he was trying harder and harder each year to put as much distance as possible between himself and them, but it never worked. During his many years at the BBC, he spent countless hours with the dearly departed David Oates and Jimmy Armfield dissecting each and every miserable result, Oatsey cursing and Jim smiling benevolently. Jimmy had seen it all before.

It's not all about Blackpool FC and football, though. Roy is also a season-ticket holder at OGC Nice – another club that seems to delight in underachievement – and has many other interests. So far, he has had 12 books published, from a dark novel of murder to the life of Mary, Queen of Scots; from behind the scenes in North Korea to the World Water Speed Record, and also on his 'other' sporting hero (alongside Alan Suddick), James Hunt.

Living in Nice means he's away from the hurly-burly of Blackpool and Bloomfield Road, but his heart is, and always will be, tangerine. Long may that continue.

PICTURE CREDITS

ACKNOWLEDGEMENTS

I didn't want to write another Blackpool FC book. I'd done two and they are hard work and I had nothing else to say, but you never say never. So here we are again, this time a biography, a crazy dash around history and a fans' view of the club we love.

I wanted this one to be different and not a season-by-season definition of the highs and lows, but rather to race around the years like a pinball. A stream of consciousness, a conversation we might have in the pub discussing our favourite player or least-liked manager – and there are 'fantasy' sequences that hopefully give a sense of the time they describe, plus quotes and interviews taken from genuine sources.

With those sequences, I admit to taking a certain artistic licence. The scene describing Jimmy Hampson getting off the train at Kirkham didn't actually happen, but he did *want* to as there were hundreds of supporters waiting for him.

Elsewhere, the supporter at the 1953 Cup final is a real person who told me his story years ago. He vividly remembered the three Bolton ladies sat a few rows ahead and their demeanour changing as Blackpool took control at the end. His thoughts and his conversation with his friend are pretty close to the reality.

The 'new Kop' story in 1930 is entirely fictional, as is the thought process going through Les Shannon's mind in the catastrophic defeat by Chelsea in 1970. I hope no one is offended.

Of course, the meeting with the original directors is another moment of fiction, but the young boy who caught the number 6 bus and stood on the Kop as the Sunderland fans approached was me. I was stubborn and stupid, but I saw that stunning Mickey Walsh goal.

Finally, the opening sequence at the start of the book is an attempt to show how two teams, representing the same force, were only divided by time. I hope it registers with most of you.

The book couldn't have been written without the help of so many people. Firstly, my huge thanks to Gary and Derek at Conker Editions who read my original submission and believed in it. Other publishers showed an interest, but none seemed to share the same vision. I'm also grateful to all the fans who have contributed with pictures, articles and support and encouragement.

I hope I haven't missed anyone when crediting the articles, but I must express my deepest gratitude to John Cross, who once again came to my rescue by supplying some wonderful photos. Others who deserve a special mention are Chris Hull, Phil Harrison, Andy Bell, Peter Dix, John Walsh, Kristen Cunliffe, Chris Riedel, David Jackson

and Elgar Williams, who all contributed images used in the book.

Also, a big 'thank you' to Christine Seddon for explaining in a very informative way the boycott by the supporters. I couldn't think of a better person to write the piece, and she did it brilliantly.

Certain players took the time to answer my questions. Peter Suddaby and Brett Ormerod are two in particular, Peter especially being very chatty about his time at the club. Of course, it is the players, managers, owners, but mostly the fans who made this book. From the first few who gathered to watch a selection of men kick a ball around a tufted field, to the flat-capped men who cheered on Hampson as he broke every record, to the Woodbine-smoking men at Wembley waving hats in the air, the youngsters watching Ball and Armfield, the wrist-tied scarved hooligans who caused havoc and the stubborn and admirable fans who boycotted. This is all for you.

TEAMWORK

Grateful thanks to everyone who subscribed in advance to 'Flat Caps & Tangerine Scarves'.

1. Geoff Banting. 2. Peter Moore. 3. Steven Scobie. 4. Peter Seddon.

5. Stephen Wilson Mather. 6. Dan Salisbury. 7. Jen James.

8. Philip Harrison. 9. Duncan Long. 10. Dave Wright. 11. Peter Dix.

12. Brett Martin Summers. 13. Paul Summers. 14. Jonathan Tite.

15. Elgar & Anne Williams. 16. Bethan Jenkins. 17. Rhydian Williams.

18. Dave Tomlinson. 19. Fred Jackson. 20. Gary Ford.

21. Dad & Gary Robinson - Blackpool Loyal. 22. Sam J Mcwhinnie.

23. Chris Lowry. 24. Darren Horn. 25. Dave Horn.

26. William Edmondson. 27 Graham Butterworth. 28. Ben Johnston.

29. Gary Johnston. 30. David Turner. 31. Alban O'Brien.

32. Nick Cunliffe. 33. John Marlor. 34. Chris Marlor. 35. John Walsh.

36. Seamus Slowey. 37. Douglas Hanson. 38. Christopher Hanson.

39. Andrew Grice - The Armfield Club. 40. Jordan Hayes.

41. Jon Sutton. 42. Peter Duerden. 43. Paul Knight. 44. Colin McGown.

45. Phil Hornby. 46. Neil Holden. 47. Peter Parr @Supergrampspete.

48. Phil Corbett. 49. Ben Gandy. 50. Chris Riedel. 51. Mark Hillary.

52. Don McLeod. 53. John D Cross. 54. Dave Maddox.

55. Steve Cartmell. 56. Derek Yarwood. 57. Derek Duckworth.

58. Alan Beauchamp. 59. Rodney Beauchamp. 60. Ethan Creighton.

61. John Creighton. 62. Jim Scrivener. 63. John Woodman.

64. Leanne Smith. 65. Steve Moore. 66. Simon Fielding.

67. Jarrod & Ethan Lane. 68. Michael Copley. 69. Peter Rushton.

70. Simon P Jones. 71. Nigel Moore. 72. Bob Stinger. 73. Martin Bryce.

74. Carl T. Goode. 75. Thomas Black. 76. David Johnson.

77. Ian Rayner. 78. Graham Eccles. 79. Mark Scholes.

80. Andy Monkman. 81. David Holden. 82. Peter Gillatt. 83. Andy Holt.

84. Dave Wiggins. 85. Sarah Jane Robinson. 86. Ant Stephen.

87. Chad Bentley. 88. Craig Harrop. 89. Mark Chapman.

90. Ian Stanier. 91. Bob Wilson. 92. Gareth Lougher.

93. Stephen Hellewell. 94. Sam Brown. 95. Robert Brown.
96. Howard Webster. 97. Darren Ing. 98. Ian Carden. 99. David Allan.
100. MG Whittard. 101. Tony Butcher. 102. Mick Whitworth.
103. Ben Wareham. 104. Steve Yarwood. 105. Mark Harrison.
106. Bernard Harrison. 107. Paul Harrison. 108. Bernard Sibbald.
109. Mark Potter. 110. Wayne Atkinson. 111. Tim & George Sparks.
112. Neil Hunter. 113. Ian Hunter. 114. Mike Eastwood.
115. Richard Robinson. 116. Nanda Marchant. 117. Adele Scarlett.
118. Andy Taylor. 119. Philip Walsh. 120. Mark Hempleman.
121. David Hale. 122. Tim Fielding. 123. Andy Cocker.
124. Michael Cocker. 125. Pete Battle. 126. Phil Armitage.
127. Rodney Palmer. 128. Kevin Ogden. 129. Stuart Ockwell.
130. Michael Melody. 131. Cliff Smith. 132. Steve Day.
133. Lee Timmins. 134. Andy Dickman. 135. Steve Rowland.
136. Steve Fisher. 137. Gary Elston. 138. Philippa Mercer.
139. Jim Warwick. 140. Chris Parsonage. 141. Stephen Bennett.
142. Pete Farrow. 143. Tony Matthews. 144. Bob Boardman.
145. Daz Jennings. 146. Chris Harrison. 147. Thomas McKenna.
148. Paul Knowles. 149. Simon Turner. 150. Nichola Gillett.
151. Keith Jenkinson. 152. Patrick Jenkinson. 153. Matthew Jenkinson.
154. Max Jenkinson. 155. George Dunmore. 156. Andrew Bennett.
157. Gareth Driver. 158. Oliver Peat. 159. Peter Mather.
160. Keith Jenkinson. 161. Rob Walker. 162. Chris Walker.
163. Ian & Ted Howe. 164. Peter Bowley. 165. Karen McGuinness.
166. David Campbell. 167. Alan Dickinson. 168. Thomas Dickinson.
169. Laraine Stranex. 170. Andrew Landau. 171. John Millburn.
172. Damian Walsh. 173. Mark Atkinson. 174. Harry Horrocks.
175. David Jagger. 176. Andrew Yule. 177. David Yule.
178. Andy Dyer. 179. Christopher Blackburn. 180. John Campbell.
181. Christopher Heaney. 182. Simon Heaney. 183. David Wakeford.
184. Gavin Day.